PUBLIC OPINION
in the
UNITED STATES

PUBLIC OPINION
in the
UNITED STATES

Studies of Race, Religion, Gender, and Issues that Matter

Rita J. Simon and
Mohamed Alaa Abdel-Moneim

Routledge
Taylor & Francis Group

LONDON AND NEW YORK

First published 2010 by Transaction Publishers

2 Park Square, Milton Park, Abingdon, Oxfordshire OX14 4RN
711 Third Avenue, New York, NY 10017

*Routledge is an imprint of the Taylor & Francis Group, an informa
business*

First issued in paperback 2017

Copyright © 2010 Taylor & Francis

Library of Congress Catalog Number: 2009036452

Library of Congress Cataloging-in-Publication Data

Simon, Rita J. (Rita James), 1931-
    Public opinion in the United States : studies of race, religion, gender,
    and issues that matter / Rita J. Simon and Mohamed Alaa Abdel-Mo-
    neim.
        p. cm.
    Includes bibliographical references and index.
    ISBN 978-1-4128-1157-6
        1. Public opinion--United States. 2. United States--Social condi-
    tions--Public opinion. I. Abdel-Moneim, Mohamed Alaa. II. Title.
HN90.P8S553 2009
303.3'80973--dc22
                                                                2009036452
    ISBN 13: 978-1-4128-1157-6 (hbk)
    ISBN 13: 978-1-138-51379-2 (pbk)

To my mother, Amany, with all my love and respect
-Mohamed Alaa Abdel-Moneim

Contents

Introduction

Public Opinion in the United States
A Mirror of Social Contention and Change

The purpose of this book is to follow developments in American society since World War II through the lens of public opinion. We report and assess national public opinion poll data from 1945 to 2008. The targets are opinions vis-à-vis African-Americans, Jews, Muslim-Americans, gays and lesbians, immigration, abortion, and affirmative action. For some of the issues, poll data may not be available until later in the 20th century, but we shall report national data for each topic from the first survey until the present time, 2008.

Through these surveys we are exploring whether the society, for example, developed faster than the Supreme Court decisions, how it processed and responded to the race riots of the 1950s and 1960s, and how the war in Vietnam shaped new perspectives on issues such as race, citizenship rights, and the role of the individual. After analyzing the developments of public opinion toward the issues identified above, the following chapters will start by introducing political, social, or international events that we believe were critical in setting the stage for directing public opinion in each decade since the end of WWII. We then relate this to public opinion survey results during that decade.

Overall, our aim is to provide a portrait of American society and assess how it has changed or remained the same over the last sixty plus years. Are Americans more or less prejudiced against blacks, Jews, and Muslims than they were in earlier years? Have their views on immigration, affirmative action, and abortion changed and if they have in what direction? Do all groups in our society, e.g., men and women, rich and poor, more and less educated, and secular versus religious share the same views? Again if there are differences, what directions do those differences take?

In the end we shall be able to describe how similar or different American society looks in 2008 than it did in the post-World War II era and offer some glimpses into the direction it is moving. We are very much aware that in 2008, the American people elected their first African-American President.

1

Public Opinion toward African-Americans

As of the 2006 census data, African-Americans, at 36.7 million people, comprised 12 percent of the population.

The median age for the black community is 31 years. Four out of five black adults finished high school, compared with only one third in 1970 and 19 percent of black adults twenty-five years and older completed college. In 1970 only 4 percent had completed college. In 2005, 45 percent of black college graduates were married, among those without a high school diploma, 24 percent were married. The distribution of household incomes in black families between 1970 and 2006 is shown below.

The figures below indicate the black median income as a percentage of the white median income for 1976 to 2006.

We note that there has been little change over the past thirty years.

Table 1.1
Black Household Income: 1970 to 2006

	<$15,000 %	$15K-25K %	$25K-35K %	$35K-$50K %	$50K-75K %	$75K-100K %	$100K %
2006	24.4	15.2	13.5	14.8	15.2	7.7	9.1
2000	22.3	15.2	12.8	16.0	16.6	8.2	8.8
1990	31.7	14.8	12.6	14.3	15.0	6.0	5.7
1980	32.3	18.4	13.,3	14.5	13.5	5.2	2.7
1970	31.8	18.7	15.0	16.6	12.3	4.1	1.6

Note: Figures are percent of total for that year. Earlier years adjusted to 2006 dollars. Blacks include Hispanic blacks.
Source: U.S. Bureau Census "Income, Poverty and Health Insurance Coverage in the United States, 2006."

Table 1.2
**Black Median Income as a Percentage of the
White Median Income from 1976 to 2006**

Year	%
2006	61
2000	65
1997	62
1986	56
1976	58

Although blacks make up only 12 percent of the population, they comprise 40 percent of the persons incarcerated in state and federal prisons. In 2005 blacks were about twice as likely as whites to be a victim of a crime.

We turn now to the public opinion data on the attitudes of white Americans toward blacks from 1945 to 2008.

National Poll Data

One of the earliest questions to appear on national polls was:

"In general do you think Negroes are as intelligent as white people; that is, can they learn just as well if they are given the same education (and training) (NORC)?"

Yes %	No %	Don't Know %
42	48	10

The last time that item appeared on a national survey was twenty-one years later, in 1963. At that time, 76 percent answered "yes." The same item appeared on national surveys at least four other times over the twenty-one-year period, with results as shown in Table 1.3.

Unfortunately, there is a gap of ten years during a period when some important institutional changes were occurring on this issue (between 1946 and 1956), which makes it difficult to trace the rate of opinion change. We note that in the four years between 1942 and 1946 (that is, during much of World War II), there was an increase of 11 percent. If we assume that opinions changed at about the same rate for the following decade, we would arrive at a figure close to the 77 percent that is

Table 1.3
Percent Saying Negroes Are as Intelligent As Whites (1942-1963) (NORC)

Year	Percent
1942	41
1944	42
1946	52
1956	77
1963	76

reported for 1956. It is clear, however, from the percentages shown that the attitudes of white Americans shifted noticeably in the direction of greater acceptance of an inherent-equality doctrine.

The next question we examine asked, "How did the changes in attitudes as manifested by the responses reported in Table 1.3 influence public attitudes in other spheres, especially in the controversy over integrated versus segregated schools?"

On the issue of school desegregation it is possible to trace changes in white attitudes both to the principle of integration and to the degree of acceptance of change in behavior that followed from the *Brown v. Board of Education* Supreme Court decision. The following item, which was included on at least five national surveys between 1942 and 1965, goes to the matter of principle. The distribution of responses indicates a consistent and steady increase in the percentage of respondents who said they approved of whites and Negroes going to the same school.

"Do you think white students and Negro students should go to the same schools or to separate schools (NORC)?"

A few weeks after the Supreme Court ruled on the illegality of segregated public-school systems, the public was asked whether it approved or disapproved of the Court's decision. The data in Table 1.5 show that in 1954, the public response was split: 54 percent indicated approval; 41 percent disapproval; and 5 percent said they had no opinion. Between 1954 and 1961, the distribution of responses to this item remained relatively stable. The proportion who indicated approval fluctuated between 54 and 62 percent.[1] The percentages in Table 1.5 also show that support for the Court's decision matched closely the percentages who supported integrated schools during those same years.

Table 1.4
"Do You Think White Students and Negro Students
Should Go to the Same Schools or to Separate Schools (NORC)?"

1942	1956	1963	1964*	1965
30%	49%	62%	63%	67%

*In 1964, when a national sample of Negroes was asked this question, 92 percent answered "the same school."

Table 1.5
Percent Approving of School-Desegregation Decision, 1954-1961 (AIPO)

July 1954	54
May 1955	55
Feb. 1956	56
Jan. 1957	62
Aug. 1957	56
Sept. 1957	54
Oct. 1957	57
July 1959	57
June 1961	61

It is ironic that in 1956, when 77 percent of those polled answered that they believed Negroes were as intelligent as white people, only 49 percent (comparing responses to the two items during the same period, 1956) approved of Negro children attending the same schools as white children (NORC). When the item on the Supreme Court's decision on school desegregation was asked only of *southern* whites, the percent who approved did not go above 20 percent at any time between 1954 and 1961 (AIPO).[2]

Responses to the following item indicated even more dramatically the public's lack of support for the implications of the Court's decision on school desegregation:

"Would you object to having your children attend a school where the *majority* of pupils are Negroes (AIPO)?"

Table 1.6
Percent Opposed to Child in School Where Majority Is Negro. 1954-1970 (AIPO)

Year	(%) Outside South	(%) South Only
1954	45	81
1958	57	82
1959	57	83
1963	53	83
1965	52	76
1966	59	60
1969	53	54
1970	51	69

Table 1.6 shows that in the sixteen years, from the time of the initial pronouncement of the doctrine until the period when Northerners, especially those living in large urban centers, realized that *de facto* segregation was as much a target of the Court's subsequent decisions as were the official policies of the southern states, the public became *less* rather than more supportive of the doctrine of "integration with all deliberate speed." By 1966, the trends were such that there was practically no difference in responses between the North and the South. But by 1970, when the prospect that busing in the South would become more widespread and involve much greater numbers of children, there was again a divergence of opinion, with southern responses more anti-integration than northern.

When the same item was asked, but instead of a "majority" of Negro pupils the proportion was "half," the percent who objected dropped from 39 in 1954 to 24 in 1970 in the North and from 81 to 43 in the South. When the number of Negro children in the question was "a few," the percent in the North dropped from 13 to 6 and in the South from 72 to 16 for the same time period (AIPO).

Closely related to the issue of how quickly and how extensively a local school is to be integrated is the problem of how it is to be done. Thus far, the busing of children across school districts is the technique used most often. It is a technique that even in 1970, more than a decade and a half since the Supreme Court's initial decision on the topic, is strongly opposed by more than 75 percent of those questioned. In March 1970, 81 percent said they opposed "the busing of Negro and white school children from one school district to another" (AIPO); and eight months later, in reviewing the results of local referendums on this issue, the *Gallup Opinion Index* reported that 78 percent had indicated their opposition to "busing school children in order to achieve a better racial balance" (AIPO).

The responses to these items—attitudes toward the integration decision, feelings about having one's children attend a school with a majority of Negro children, and the busing of children across school districts—point up a basic dilemma in American society. In principle, almost two thirds of the respondents said that they supported integration. But the closer to home and the more realistic the implications of school integration became, the less willing were white Americans to go along, especially those who said they favored integration in principle.

Transportation, Housing, and Employment

In other areas involving public facilities such as transportation, housing, and employment opportunities, there have been dramatic shifts in attitudes that indicate continued and widespread support for civil-rights legislation. Beginning in 1942 and periodically over the next two decades, when asked whether there should be separate sections for Negroes in streetcars and buses, the public exhibited an increase in a pro-civil-rights direction of almost 100 percent from 44 to 79 percent between 1942 and 1963, as shown in Table 1.7.

On the housing issue, when asked whether it would make any difference to them if a Negro with just as much income and education moved into their block, the public responded consistently in a direction that supported civil rights. In October 1966 on Table 1.8 we note a sharp

Table 1.7
Percent Disapproving of Separate Sections in Buses
1942-1963 (AIPO and NORC)

Year	(%)	
1942	44	(NORC)
1945	49	(AIPO)
1949	50	(AIPO)
1956	59	(NORC)
1961	65	(AIPO)
1963	79	(NORC)

drop between 1965 and 1966: only 49 percent said they did not object to having a Negro living next door. This figure is even lower than that shown for 1956. The acceptance of Negro neighbors is obviously a more sensitive index of social equality than is agreement that Negroes ought to be able to share the same section of a train or bus. In the items that concerned school desegregation, many more respondents, especially those living in the North, favored desegregation until it involved their own children, especially if their children were likely to have more than minimal exposure to Negroes. A similar pattern occurred with respect to housing. The drop in white respondents who were willing to reduce "social distance" may have been a reaction to the civil disturbances that occurred during 1964 and 1965 in which Negroes living in northern urban districts participated.

What the data presented thus far have shown was a willingness to ver-balize support for civil rights in the abstract and insofar as they affected impersonal matters. But greater intimacy, as manifested by neighborhood integration and *de facto* school integration, was still not desired or even acceptable to a majority of white Americans in the North or South.

Following the end of World War II, there was a concerted effort by President Truman, civil-rights organizations, and liberal members of the Congress to gain enactment of a law guaranteeing fair employment opportunities. In 1945, 43 percent favored a law that would require em-ployers to hire a person if he qualified for the job, regardless of his race or color (AIPO). From 1944 to 1946, between 42 and 47 percent said that they thought Negroes should have as good a chance as white people to get any kind of job (NORC).

When asked how far the federal government should go in requir-ing employers to hire people without regard to race, religion, color, or

Table 1.8
Percent Saying It Would Make No Difference if a
Negro Moved into Their Block, 1942-1966 (NORC and HAR)

Year		(%)
1942	(NORC)	35
1956	(NORC)	51
1963	(NORC)	61
1965	(HAR)	62
1966	(HAR)	49

nationality, only about one third of the respondents favored direct and significant federal intervention, as indicated by Table 1.9. The largest category supported no federal action at all.

In the early 1950s, the public was asked to choose between state and federal intervention to ensure fair employment policies. About the same proportion who had answered "None of the Way" in Table 1.9 indicated that they favored having each state decide for itself. (Presumably, that meant that each state could decide not to act at all.) In 1952 and 1953, when asked whether there should be a national law requiring employers to hire people without regard to color or race, or whether the issue should be left to each state to decide for itself, about the same proportion (32-34 percent), who had answered "All the Way" on Table 1.9 favored a national law, and about the same proportion (45-41 percent) who said "None of the Way" advocated "leaving it up to the states" (AIPO). In reviewing the level of responses to the series of items concerning federal intervention in providing more equal employment opportunities for Negroes, we note that no more than 43 percent favored such action between 1944 and 1953.

A decade later, which by then was the third year of the Kennedy administration, each of these items appeared again on national polls. The changes in public opinion as represented by the level of responses to these same items are dramatic. For example, when asked in 1963 whether Negroes should have as good a chance as white people to get any kind of job, 82 percent answered "yes" (HAR). This figure is an increase of almost 50 percent since 1944 and 1946. When asked about a national law requiring employers to hire people without regard to color or race, 86 percent said they favored such a national law (NORC). This is an increase of over 100 percent since 1950. By the 1960s, on the matter of employment opportunities, the trend was clearly and strongly in favor of civil rights for Negroes.

Table 1.9
Federal Intervention to Require Nondiscriminatory Hiring. 1948-1950 (AIPO)
(In Percent)

Year	All the Way	None of the Way	Depends on Type of Work	Leave to State Government	No Opinion
1948	32	45	7	2	14
1949	34	45	5	2	14
1950	34	41	14	*	11

* In 1950, this choice was not given.

The direction and level of responses to these items are consistent with the responses to items involving housing, public transportation, and education.[3] On each of these issues, the more distant or abstract the problem, the greater the shift of opinion toward a pro-civil rights position. The provisions in the Civil Rights Act of 1964 include many of the topics about which public opinion had shifted from the 1940s and 1950s to the middle 1960s. The frustrations that the Truman administration experienced in gaining passage of a civil rights law bore fruit a decade and a half later in the Kennedy-Johnson era.

Table 1.10, based on responses to a national survey conducted in December 1963, is a good summary of white attitudes as of that date. The range of pro-integration responses between Items 1 and 8 is consistent with the impressions gained from the item-by-item analyses, which are that a high proportion of white Americans support impersonal and institutionalized expressions of tolerance but that more intimate contacts, such as those manifested by gestures of friendship or neighborliness, invitations to one's home, or marriage are still resisted or disapproved of by most whites.

Demonstrations in the 1960s

Many observers of the national scene have described the changes in American society from the relatively silent, stable 1950s to the riot-ridden 1960s as near-revolutionary in their pervasiveness and intensity. In the area of civil rights especially, the 1960s was a period of turbulence and social change. Sheatsley quotes a Gallup release in October 1963 as follows:[4]

> the question of race relations has been consistently cited by Americans as the most important problem facing the Unite States, "except when it has been temporarily displaced by some international crisis such as Vietnam."

In this section, we examine, and where possible compare, responses of white and black citizens to the demonstrations, marches, riots, looting, and other activities that marked this new era in civil rights.

In 1961 the American public was asked:

> Do you feel demonstrations of Negroes have helped more or hurt more the advancement of Negro rights (AIPO and HAR)?

This item appeared in more or less the same form at least once a year from 1961 through 1967 with the results shown in table 1.11. The data show a rather consistent trend against support for demonstrations by Negroes on the part of the white community on the grounds that the

Table 1.10
Guttman Scale of Pro-Integration Sentiment, 1963

Item	Pro-Integration Percentage
1. Do you think Negroes should have as good a chance as white people to get any kind of job, or do you think white people should have the first chance at any kind of job?	82
2. Generally speaking, do you think there should be separate sections for Negroes in streetcars and buses?	77
3. Do you think Negroes should have the right to use the same parks, restaurants, and hotels as white people?	71
4. Do you think white students and Negro students should go to the same schools or to separate schools?	63
5. How strongly would you object if a member of your family wanted to bring a Negro friend home to dinner?	49
6. White people have a right to keep Negroes out of their neighborhoods if they want to, and Negroes should respect that right.	44
7. Do you think there should be laws against marriages between Negroes and whites?	36
8. Negroes shouldn't push themselves where they're not wanted.	27

Adapted from Paul B. Sheatsley, "White Attitudes Toward the Negro," Daedalus (Winter 1966), 217-237, at p. 224. Reprinted by permission of Daedalus, Journal of the American Academy of Arts and Sciences, Boston, MA, Winter, 1966. The Negro American-2. To quote Sheatsley: "The properties of a Guttman scale are such that if a person rejects one item on the scale, the chances are at least nine in ten that he will reject the items below it. Thus, those who reject the top item-equal job opportunities for Negroes—are highly unlikely to endorse any of the other items on the scale and may be considered extreme segregationists. At the other end of the scale, the 27 percent who disagree with the proposition that 'Negroes shouldn't push themselves where they're not wanted' are extremely likely to take a prointegration position on all seven of the other items."

demonstrations were "hurting more than helping" the Negroes' chances for full social and political equality.[5]

In his study of Negro attitudes "toward their own situation, the whites, the community and the civil rights movement," Gary Marx reported the responses of Negro respondents in 1964 to this parallel item:[6]

Would you say about the civil-rights demonstrations over the last few years that they have helped Negroes a great deal, helped a little, hurt a little, or a great deal?

About 56 percent answered "helped a great deal," and an additional 30 percent said "helped a little." In the same year, looking at the results in Table 1.11 we note that 21 percent of the white respondents believed that demonstrations helped more than hurt the Negroes. The differences between white and Negro opinion on what had become the strategy of the 1960s for calling attention to the situation of Negroes in the United States and for bringing about concrete improvements in their status are dramatically demonstrated by the disparity of responses to this item. The Negro respondents were almost unanimous in their belief that demonstrations helped Negroes, while only 10 percent of the whites during the same period shared that conviction. The item was asked of both the Negroes and whites in the fall of 1964, after the demonstrations and riots of the previous summer.

In the summer of 1961, the white community was asked its opinion about the "freedom rides." The question read:

Do you approve or disapprove of what the Freedom Riders are doing (AIPO)?

In that period, the main participants in the freedom rides were middle-class young people (mostly college students) from northern and southern universities. But even so 64 percent of whites polled answered that they disapproved of such activities. Two years later, 63 percent said they disapproved of the proposed civil-rights demonstration that was planned to follow the march on Washington.[7] This was the march organized by Bayard Rustin and led by Martin Luther King, Jr., in which some 200,000 persons are said to have participated. The march on Washington, the freedom rides, the lunch-counter sit-ins were all demonstrations organized and led by "responsible" middle-class white and black leaders. We had not yet entered the Black Power era, the Black Panthers were either non-existent or not visible outside the ghetto, and men with the rhetoric of a Bobbie Seale, a Rap Brown, an Eldridge Cleaver, or a Huey Newton were

Table 1.11
Percent Saying Demonstrations Hurt Negro Rights
1961-1967 (AIPO and HAR)

July 1961	(AIPO)	58
July 1963	(HAR)	65
July 1964	(AIPO)	80
July 1965	(HAR)	60
June 1966	(HAR)	68
Oct. 1966	(HAR)	86
Aug. 1967	(HAR)	89

not the organizers or the leaders of these acts of protest. Nevertheless, the white community did not support activities that, in retrospect, appear as relatively mild forays into the white establishment.[8]

During the summers of 1963 and 1964, the white community expressed the reactions shown in table 1.12 to specific activities in the "new" civil-rights campaign.

On the larger issue of how whites perceived the general status of the Negroes in American society, it is interesting to compare the level of responses to two items: the first was asked on national surveys in the 1940s and 1950s; the second, in 1967 and 1968 and again in 2001. The questions and the responses are shown in table 1.13. Up through 1968, most white people said they believe that Negroes are treated fairly, but in 2001, only a little more than a third believed blacks were treated the same as whites.

Between 1968 and 2001 the following item appeared on national polls:

Do you believe blacks are treated the same as whites in your community?

Table 1.12
White Attitude on Civil-Rights Activities, 1963-1964 (HAR)

Activity/Item	Disapproval Percentage Nationwide
Summer 1963	
Lie down in front of truck at construction sites to protest hiring discrimination	91
Sit-in at lunch counters	67
Go to jail to protest discrimination	56
Boycott products whose manufacturers don't hire enough Negroes	55
Summer 1964	
1. This summer white and Negro students are going to Mississippi to organize Negroes to vote. Do you generally approve of this move or disapprove of it?	57
2. Do people approve or disapprove of picketing of political conventions as occurred at the Cow Palace in San Francisco?	76
3. People have different views about the Negro demonstrations. Some people say the Negroes should stop their demonstrations now that they have made their point and even though some of their demands have not been met. Others say they have to continue demonstrating in order to achieve better jobs, better housing, and better schools. With which view do you agree? (Stop demonstrating.)	73

Table 1.13
Treatment of Negroes, 1944-1968 (NORC)

Item	Year	Fairly/Same as Whites (%)
1. Do you think most Negroes in the United States are being treated fairly or unfairly?	1944 1946 1956	60 66 66
2. In your opinion, how well do you think Negroes are treated in this country— the same as whites are, not very well, or badly?	1967 1968 2001	72 70 38

In 1968, 62 percent of the white respondents thought they were and in 2001, 69 percent thought they were. Over the years (in 1997, 1998, and 1999) as many as 76 percent of the white respondents thought that blacks were treated the same as whites in their community.

When asked: "Do black children have the same chance as white children to get a good education in your community?" And "Do blacks have the same chances as whites to get affordable housing in your community?" The results are shown in the charts below.

In responses to both items at least 71 percent of the white respondents and as high as 86 percent thought that blacks had the same chances as whites.

On more general themes we found that when asked: "Have black-white relations improved or gotten worse over the last year?" from 1997 through 2001 between 27 and 31 percent of white respondents believed relations had improved.

	Item 1
Year	Percent Same Chance
1962	83
1989	80
1990	83
1991	81
1995	82
1999	82
2001	80

	Item 2
Year	Percent Same Chance
1989	71
1991	74
1997	86
2001	83

When asked to "rate the state of race relations in the U.S. today" the results looked like this:

Year	Somewhat or Very Good (%)
1998	43
1999	50
2001	46

Slightly less than half rated race relations favorably.

And looking into the future when asked: "What is the likelihood that a solution to the problem of black/white relations in the United States will ever be worked out?" The responses shown below indicate that save for the years 1963 and 2001 when slightly less than half of the respondents said there will always be problems in the relations between blacks and whites, at least 53 percent and in 1995 as high as 62 percent thought there would always be problems.

Year	Will always be a Problem (%)
1963	44
1973	53
1995	62
1997	54
1998	57
1999	51
2001	45

In 2001 black respondents were asked if they believe they received unfair treatment in a variety of situations: shopping, dealing with police, in restaurants, bars, and theaters, at work, and while using public transit. The results are shown below:

Context	Unfairly Treated (%)
Shopping in a store	27
In dealing with police	21
In restaurant, bars, theaters	20
At work	19
While using public transit	5

Between a fifth and a fourth of the respondents reported unfair treatment in all of the contexts save one: public transit. Only 5 percent reported that they felt they were treated unfairly while riding on buses or trains.

What about the future of blacks? Will life be better, the same or worse. From the responses shown below, we see that in 2007 only 44 percent of blacks thought life would be better in the future. This percent is down from 57 percent in 1986 who said life would be better for them in the future. At 56 percent, more white Americans in 2007 thought life would be better for blacks than did black Americans. Gender made no difference in the black responses but education did. Blacks with less than a high school education were less likely to think life in the future would be better than did blacks with a college education, 34 v. 50 percent.

The future will be	Whites (%) 2007	Blacks (%)	
		1986	2007
Better	56	57	44
Worse	6	23	21
About the Same	32	14	31
Don't Know	6	6	4

In 2007 a majority of both blacks and whites believe that "blacks who can't get ahead are mostly responsible for their own condition." But as the figures below show, 71 percent of whites think that compared to 53 percent of blacks.

Table 1.14
Which of These Statements Comes Closer to Your Views:
Racial Discrimination Is the Main Reason Why Many Black People
Can't Get Ahead or Blacks Who Can't Get Ahead Are Mostly
Responsible for Their Own Condition....

	All adults (%)	Whites (%)	Blacks (%)	Hispanics (%)
Racial Discrimination	19	15	30	24
Blacks responsible for their own condition	66	71	53	59
Neither/Both (VOL)	9	8	14	8
Don't Know/Refused	6	6	3	9
	100	100	100	100
Number of Respondents	3,086	1,536	1,007	388

Note: Whites include only non-Hispanic whites. Blacks include only non-Hispanic blacks. Hispanics are of any race. Pew Research Center

Neither gender, education, or income made a difference: but age did. Younger blacks, those under 50, were more likely to think so than blacks over 50 years of age.

Finally on the issue of affirmative action blacks at 78 percent were most likely to favor affirmative action programs that would help black Americans get better jobs and education.

	Favor (%)
White	39
Black	78

Notes

1.   In 1970, a Harris survey reported that 61 percent said *de jure* school segregation—separate but equal schools under the law—was wrong, 18 percent disagreed (did not think it wrong), and 21 percent had no opinion. Comparing the distribution of responses in 1970 to that shown for 1961 in Table 6.5, we note that the differences are in the "disapprove" (or support for desegregation) and "no opinion" columns. The percent who approved (or who thought *de jure* segregation was wrong) show no noticeable increase for the past decade and a half.

2.   But in the same 1970 Harris survey cited above, 48 percent of the people who lived in the South said they believed *de jure* school segregation was wrong. Thus the segment of the population who shifted their opinion significantly in the direction

of greater acceptance were persons living in the area of the country most directly affected by the Court's decision.

3.   In the summer of 1964, Congress passed the Civil Rights Act that outlawed racial discrimination in hiring and firing wherever interstate commerce was involved, forbade the use of federal grants-in-aid in state programs that were racially discriminatory, outlawed racial discrimination in public accommodation, and provided federal grants for job-retraining programs and vocational education.

4.   Paul B. Sheatsley, "White Attitudes Toward the Negro," *Daedalus* (Winter 1966), p. 237.

5.   Nevertheless, when asked in the summer of 1964, "Do people have a right to demonstrate on behalf of civil rights?" 61 percent answered "yes."

6.   Gary Marx, *Protest and Prejudice*: New York: 1967, p. 15. Marx's sample consisted of Negroes who lived in metropolitan areas outside the South, plus a special sample of Negroes who lived in New York City, Chicago, Atlanta, and Birmingham.

7.   The item was asked only of the 69 percent who had indicated earlier that they had heard or read about the proposed rally (AIPO).

8.   When white attitudes toward integration were divided into four categories (highly in favor, moderately in favor, moderately opposed, and highly opposed) and respondents in each category were then asked "Do you approve or disapprove of the actions Negroes have taken to obtain civil rights?" only a majority of the whites in the "highly in favor" category expressed approval of these actions. The percentage who disapproved was: Highly in favor, 33%; Moderately in favor, 62%; Moderately opposed, 73%; Highly opposed, 89% (NORC).

2

Public Opinion toward Jews

In 1945, there were approximately 11 million Jewish people in the world. According to a survey conducted by Professor Sergio Della Pergola of the Jewish People Policy Planning Institute and the Harman Institute of Contemporary Jewry at the Hebrew University, as of 2008, there are 13.3 million Jews in the world. Jewish population growth worldwide is currently close to zero percent. From 2000 to 2001 the population of Jews worldwide increased by three-tenths of a percent, compared to an overall population growth of 1.4 percent. In 2008, 7.75 million Jews lived in the Diaspora and 4.9 percent lived in Israel. Among the Diaspora countries, following the U.S., France at 490,000 Jews has the third largest Jewish community in the world, followed by Canada at 375,000, Russia at 340,000, the United Kingdom at 295,000, Argentina at 183,000, and the Ukraine at 112,000 Jews. Percentage wise, 63 percent of the Jewish population live in the Diaspora, with 64 percent in North America, 12 percent in Europe, and 5 percent in South America, Africa, Asia, and Australia.[1]

More Jews live in the United States than in any country throughout the world—including Israel. As of 2008, there are 5.3 million Jews in the United States, 2.5 percent of the population. The Jews in the United States and the Jews in Israel together comprise 86 percent of the world's Jewish population. New York City, with 1.9 million Jews, is the world's second largest Jewish city and the largest American city. Los Angeles, with 621,000 Jews is the world's fourth largest.[2]

The first major immigration of Jewish people to the United States came from Germany following the failed revolution of 1848. In 1880, one sixth of the quarter million American Jews living in the U.S. emigrated from Eastern Europe. By 1920, about five sixths of the 4 million Jews in the U.S. were Eastern European immigrants. According to a study by Professor DellaPergola, "in the next eighty years America's

Jewish population would decline by one-third to 3.8 million if current fertility rates and migration patterns continue."[3] There are 13 Jews in the United States Senate, two are republican (Norm Coleman and Arlen Specter) and thirty in the House of Representatives, only one of whom is a republican. There are two Jewish Supreme Court Justices: Stephen Breyer and Ruth Bader Ginsburg.

National Poll Data

One of the earliest surveys, conducted in 1938, asked about Jews and their power in the United States. The same item was repeated in surveys conducted in the 1940s, the 1960s and in 1981. In 1938, 40 percent of the respondents said they believed Jews have too much power in this country. The percent believing that increased to a high of 56 and 55 percents in 1944 and 1946. In 1962, 1964, and 1981, 17, 13, and 23 percent thought Jews have too much power in this country.

From August 1940 through March 1959, respondents were asked:

"Have you heard any criticism or talk against the Jews in the last six months?"

The responses show that beginning in November 1950 the percentage who heard criticism declined sharply from over 60 percent to less than 25 percent, and in 1956 and in 1959 to 11 and 12 percent.

	Percent Yes
August 1940	46
February 1941	47
October 1941	50
December 1942	50
May 1944	62
March 1945	62
February 1946	64
November 1950	24
April 1951	16
July 1953	21
November 1954	14
November 1955	14
November 1956	11
March 1959	12

Table 2.1
Percent Saying Jews Have Too Much Power 1938-1964

Year	Percent
1938	40
1940	42
1942	46
1944	56
1946	55
1962	17
1964	13
1981	23

Table 2.2
Objectionable Qualities of Jews (OPOR and AIPO)
(In percent)*

Quality	1938	1940	1962
None mentioned	42	37	78
Greed	13	-	-
Dishonesty (In 1940 Unscrupulousness)	12	32	6
Aggressiveness	9	12	6
Clannishness	7	11	4
Lack of Culture	2	10	1
Selfishness	5	4	1
Overbearance	3	-	-
Appearance	-	4	4
Other	8	4	7
	101	114	107

*Some respondents mentioned more than one quality

In the 1930s, 1940s, and 1960s, a series of questions were asked about the admirable and objectionable qualities that characterized Jews in this country. Between 1938 and 1940, 42 and 37 percent of the respondents did not indicate any objectionable quality. In 1962, 78 percent of those surveyed did not mention any objectionable qualities. In 1938 and 1940, the qualities most often mentioned by a quarter and a third of the respondents were greed and dishonesty.

When asked about the admirable qualities that characterized Jews (and this question also appeared on a national survey in 2002) 49, 42, and 56 percent did not mention any admirable quality. During those years ability in business or finance was the quality most frequently mentioned, followed by racial and religious loyalty.

In 2002, the responses showed a very different portrait. For example, 80 percent answered "Jews place a strong emphasis on the importance of family life." Sixty-nine percent said Jews have contributed much to the cultural life of Americans.

In 1981, a national survey asked respondents to indicate whether they thought the following qualities about Jews were "probably true" or "probably false." They could also answer that they were "not sure." The responses show that between 60 and 81 percent of the respondents thought the qualities were probably true.

Between 32 percent and 10 percent thought such negative attributes as "Jews are always stirring up trouble with their ideas," "Jews are more loyal to Israel than the U.S.," and "Jews have too much power in the U.S." were probably true.

Table 2.3
Admirable Qualities of Jews (OPOR and AIPO)
(Percent)*

Quality	1938	1940	1962
None mentioned	49	42	56
Ability in business and finance	13	19	13
Racial or religious loyalty	12	17	16
Loyalty to wife and family	8	10	4
Intellectual attainments	7	8	5
Persistence, determination, ambition	6	9	7
Thrift, financial independence	5	-	3
Kindness, generosity, charitableness	4	-	4
Other	5	10	2
Total	109	115	110

*Some mentioned more than one quality

Table 2.4
Admirable Qualities 2002

Qualities	Percent
Jews place a strong emphasis on the importance of family life.	80
Jews have contributed much to the cultural life of Americans.	69
Jews have a special commitment to social justice and civil rights.	58
Jews have played a vital role in making sure the U.S. is a positive, moral force in world affairs.	53

Table 2.5
Beliefs about Jews among Non-Jews in 1981
(Percent)

	Probably true	Probably false	Not sure
Jews are usually hard working people.	81	6	13
Jews have a strong faith in God.	71	8	21
Jews are warm and friendly people.	64	10	26
Jews are just as honest as other businessmen.	60	17	23

Between 1964 and 2002 several items were (shown in Table 2.6) included on what has become known as the Anti-Semitic Index.

For most of the items, the percentage indicating anti-Semitic responses dropped. For example, "Jews are more willing than others to use shady practices to get what they want," dropped from 48 to 19 percent; "Jews have a lot of irritating traits," declined from 48 to 20 percent; "Jews always like to be at the head of things," declined from 63 to 35 percent; "Jews don't care what happens to anyone but their own kind," dropped from 30 to 16 percent; and "The trouble with Jewish businessmen is that they are so shrewd and tricky other people don't have a fair chance in competition," dropped from 40 to 17 percent. Only one item, "Do you think Jews have too much power in the US," increased to 20 percent from 13 percent in 1964.

Table 2.6
Anti-Semitic Index
(Percent)

Statement	1964	1969	1981	1992	1998	2002
1. Do you think Jews have too much power in the U.S.	13	11	23	31	11	20
2. Do you think Jews have too much power in the business world.	33	26	37	24	16	24
3. Jews are more willing than others to use shady tactics to get what they want.	48	28	33	21	13	19
4. Jews are more loyal to Israel than to America.	39	29	48	35	31	33
5. Jews are not as honest as other businessmen.	30	30	22	16	10	14
6. Jews have a lot of irritating traits.	48	30	28	22	14	20
7. International banking is pretty much controlled by Jews.	55	35	43	Not asked	Not asked	Not asked
8. Jews don't care what happens to anyone but their own kind.	30	40	21	16	9	16
9. Jews always like to be at the head of things.	63	42	52	39	33	35
10. Jews stick together too much.	58	52	53	51	57	50
11. The trouble with Jewish businessmen is that they are so shrewd and tricky other people don't have a chance in competition.	40	54	27	19	14	17
Asked in 1992, 1998, and 2002 instead of #7 "Jews have too much control/influence on Wall St."				27	16	20

In a May-June 2003, CNN/USA Today/Gallup poll the public was asked:
Do you think that anti-Semitism, or prejudice against Jewish people, is currently:

Table 2.7
"Do You Think That Anti-Semitism, or Prejudice against Jewish People Is Currently....?"

Choices	Percent
A very serious problem	9
Somewhat of a problem	48
Not much of a problem	30
Not a problem at all	9

We see that 57 percent believe it is a very serious or a somewhat serious problem. Non-whites at 16 percent are twice as likely as whites at 8 percent to see it as a serious problem.

When asked: "Do you agree or disagree that virtually all positions of influence in the United States are open to Jews?" the results looked like this:

Table 2.8
"Do You Agree or Disagree That Virtually All Positions of Influence in the United States Are Open to Jews?" (Percent)

Agree	59
Disagree	34

We also found that:

- Sixty-seven percent of men and 52 percent of women believe Jews have access to influential positions;
- Sixty-two percent of whites agree that Jews can gain positions of influence, while only 49 percent of non-whites agree;
- By a 68 percent to 48 percent margin, Americans who attended college are more likely than those with a high school education or less to say that Jewish people have access to influential positions in the United States;
- Republicans (68 percent) are more likely to say that Jews have access to influential positions than are independents (61 percent) and democrats (50 percent).

As responses to the following item indicate, Americans seem very willing to accept a Jew as president of the United States.

Would you vote for a Jewish candidate for president if your party nominated one?

Yes   89 percent

On other specific issues that were asked on national surveys from 1938 through 1962 we see that the responses consistently shifted from negative to positive.

"Would it make a difference to you if a prospective employee were Jewish?"

	Percent	
1940	43	Would prefer not to have a Jewish employee or coworker whom they would have to meet with on a more or less regular basis
1962	6	

"Should colleges limit the number of Jews they admit?"

Percent	Yes
1938	26
1962	4

"How would you feel about marrying a Jew?"

	Percent Would definitely not marry a Jew
1950	57
1962	37

"Suppose a Jewish family were going to move in next door to you. Would you say you wouldn't like it at all, or that you wouldn't like it but it wouldn't matter too much or that it wouldn't make any difference to you?"

	Percent Would not like it at all	Wouldn't make any difference
1950	10	69
1953	7	80
1954	3	88
1955	5	87
1956	5	86
1959	2	86
1962	3	95

Thus in 1962, 95 percent of the respondents said it would not make any difference to him/her if a Jewish family moved in next door.

A 2005 national survey of American attitudes toward Jews found that 14 percent of Americans hold views about Jews that are "unquestionably anti-Semitic," compared to 17 percent reported in 2002. In 1998, 12 percent and in 1992, 20 percent held such views.

In the 2005 survey, 35 percent of foreign born Hispanics and 36 percent of African Americans compared to only 9 percent of whites held strong anti-Semitic beliefs.

In the October 2007 survey of American attitudes toward Jews in America, 15 percent of the respondents reported views that are "unquestionably anti-Semitic."

The 2007 survey also found that 31 percent of Americans believe Jews are more loyal to Israel than America. In 1992, 35 percent, in 1998, 31 percent, in 2002, 33 percent and in 2005, 33 percent held such views.

Other items on the survey showed the following results.

Table 2.9
"Do You Believe Jews Were Responsible for the Death of Christ?"

Year	Percent Yes
2007	27
2005	30
2002	25

Table 2.10
"Do You Believe Jews Have Too Much Power in the United States?"

Year	Percent Yes
2007	15
2005	15

Table 2.11
"Do You Believe Jews Have Too Much Power in the Business World?"

Year	Percent Yes
2007	20
2005	19

Table 2.12
Anti-Semitic Opinion Based on Educational Level

Education	Percent Anti-Semitic Opinion
High School degree or less	21
College degree	10
Post-graduate degrees	8

Examining the responses of African Americans to the 2007 survey the results show that 32 percent held strong anti-Semitic opinions as opposed to 10 percent of white Americans and 15 percent of Hispanics born in the U.S.

Concerning demographic characteristics, men at 18 percent are more likely than women at 13 percent to hold anti-Semitic beliefs.

As the following results indicate, the more educated a person is, the less likely he or she is to hold anti-Semitic views.

Concluding on a positive note, the survey also found that a majority of Americans hold Jews in high regard on many issues as shown by the responses reported below:

- 55 percent believe that Jews have special commitments to social justice and civil rights;
- 65 percent agree that Jews contribute much to the cultural life of America;
- 79 percent see as positive Jewish emphasis on the importance of family life.

Notes

1.   Survey conducted by Professor Sergio Della Pergola, Jewish People Policy Planning Institute and the Harman Institute of Contemporary Jewry at the Hebrew University. Reported in *Jerusalem Post,* September 18, 2008, page 8.
2.   United States of America. (anti-Semitism), *Anti-Semitism Worldwide,* Annual 1998 issue.
3.   *http://simpletoremembercom.*

3

Public Opinion toward the Muslim-American Community

As of 2008 there are between five and six million Muslims in the United States. California, New York, and Illinois account for almost half (44.4 percent) of the Muslims in the country. About two thirds are foreign born, most have immigrated since 1990. Of the roughly one third who are native, the majority are converts and African American.

About 79 percent of all Muslims in the United States are between 16 and 65 years of age. The average household size is 4.9 persons. Twenty-four percent hold a bachelor's degree. Professionally, about 10 percent work in engineering and computers, 8 percent are employed in medical related fields and 4 percent are employed in the financial field. A 1998 Illinois study reported that Muslim Americans have an average household income of $53,500.[1]

There are 165 Islamic schools in the United States, 843 Mosques and Islamic centers, 426 associations, and 89 publications.

We turn now to national poll data on public attitudes toward the American Muslim community.

National Poll Data

The first national survey on American attitudes toward the Muslim American community was conducted in December 2004 by the Media & Society Research Group at Cornell University. Among the items included were the following shown in Table 3.1.

Support for restrictions on Muslim Americans also varies by party affiliation, degree of fear of a terrorist attack, and personal religiosity. In addition, support for restrictions also varies by level of attention to TV news. The following table provides the percentage of respondents agreeing with each statement by political party affiliation.

Table 3.1
Public Support for Restrictions on Muslim Americans

Statement	% Agreed
All Muslim Americans should be required to register their whereabouts with the federal government.	27
Mosques should be closely monitored and surveilled by U.S. law enforcement agencies.	26
U.S. government agencies should profile citizens as potential threats based on being Muslim or having Middle Eastern heritage.	22
Muslim civic and volunteer organizations should be infiltrated by undercover law enforcement agents to keep watch on their activities and fundraising.	29
Agreed with none of the statements.	48
Agreed with at least one of the statements.	44
Agreed with one statement only.	15
Agreed with two of the statements.	11
Agreed with three of the statements.	9
Agreed with all four statements.	9

Source: Media and Society Research Group, Cornell University, page 6 (Table 7).

Table 3.2
Restrictions on Muslim Americans by Party (Percent Agree)

Statement	Rep	Ind	Dem
All Muslim Americans should be required to register their whereabouts.	40	17	24
Mosques should be closely monitored.	34	24	22
U.S. government agencies should profile Muslim citizens.	34	15	17
Muslim civic and volunteer organizations should be infiltrated.	41	27	21

Source: Media & Society Research Group, Cornell University, page 6 (Table 8).

Agreement with each type of restriction on Muslim Americans varies by party affiliation. For example, 40 percent of republicans agree that Muslim Americans should register their whereabouts and law enforcement agents should infiltrate Muslim volunteer and civic organizations compared to roughly a quarter of democrats.

Table 3.3
Public Support for Restrictions on
Muslim Americans by Level of Fear (Percent Agree)

Statement	Low Fear	High Fear
All Muslim Americans should be required to register their whereabouts.	24	37
Mosques should be closely monitored.	21	42
U.S. government agencies should profile Muslim citizens.	19	31
Muslim civic and volunteer organizations should be infiltrated.	25	42

Source: Media & Society Research Group, Cornell University, page 6 (Table 9).

The following responses show the percentage of respondents agreeing with each statement by level of fear of a terrorist attack.

For each type of restriction, respondents with a high level of fear of terrorist attack are significantly more likely to agree than are those who have a lower level of fear. The gap in support is most wide for the surveillance of mosques (21 percent vs. 42 percent) and the infiltration of Muslim civic and volunteer organizations (25 percent vs. 42 percent).

A similar pattern emerges when considering variations in support for restrictions across respondents with different levels of personal religiosity. The data show the percentage of respondents agreeing with each type of restriction by level of personal religiosity.

Table 3.4
Public Support for Restrictions on Muslim Americans by Personal Religiosity
(Percent Agree)

Statement	Level of Religiosity		
	Low	Moderate	High
All Muslim Americans should be required to register their whereabouts.	15	30	42
Mosques should be closely monitored.	13	33	34
U.S. Government agencies should profile citizens based on being Muslim.	16	24	29
Muslim civic and volunteer organizations should be infiltrated.	19	33	40

Table 3.5
Opinion of Muslim-Americans

	Favorable %	Unfavorable %	(VOL.) DK/Ref %	(N)**
Total	55	25	20=100	(1000)
Sex				
Male	54	28	18	(477)
Female	55	21	24	(523)
Race				
White	53	25	22	(818)
Non-white	61	22	17	(173)
Black	64	26	10	(109)
Hispanic*	52	26	22	(63)
Race and Sex				
White Men	53	30	17	(391)
White Women	54	20	26	(427)
Age				
Under 30	62	25	13	(158)
30-49	57	22	21	(350)
50-64	54	25	21	(275)
65+	40	30	30	(202)
Sex and Age				
Men under 50	58	27	15	(252)
Women under 50	59	20	21	(256)
Men 50+	47	30	23	(222)
Women 50+	50	24	26	(255)
Education				
College Grad.	65	15	20	(354)
Some College	63	17	20	(236)
High School Grad.	45	33	22	(322)
<H.S. Grad.	41	37	22	(84)
Family Income				
$75,000+	63	21	16	(240)
$50.000-$74.999	54	27	19	(155)
$30,000-$49,999	52	24	24	(205)
$20,000-$29,999	48	23	29	(91)
<$20,000	55	28	17	(150)

Table 3.5 (cont)

Region				
East	60	20	20	(154)
Midwest	53	29	18	(248)
South	54	27	19	(389)
West	53	20	27	(209)
Religious Affiliation				
Total White Protestant	53	26	21	(452)
Evangelical	53	29	18	(257)
Non-Evangelical	53	23	24	(195)
White Catholic	61	17	22	(156)
Black Protestant	67	28	5	(71)
Secular	50	22	28	(134)
Party ID				
Republican	48	30	22	(329)
Democrat	61	21	18	(315)
Independent	55	25	20	(282)
Party and Ideology				
Conservative Republican	46	37	17	(213)
Moderate/Liberal Rep.	57	19	24	(106)
Conservative/Mod. Dem.	59	23	18	(207)
Liberal Democrat	70	19	11	(96)

*The designation Hispanic is unrelated to the white-black categorization.

**Sample size applies to "opinion of Muslim-Americans" results. Sample size for "Opinion of Islam" results at least twice the size.

Question: Would you say you have a generally favorable or unfavorable opinion of Islam (...the Muslim religion)?

Is your overall opinion of Muslim Americans very favorable, mostly favorable, mostly unfavorable, or very unfavorable?

Source: Pew Research Center for the People & the Press and Pew Forum on Religion & Public Life. July 2005 Religion and Public Life Survey, Final Topline. July 7-17, 2005. N=2000.

Approximately 40 percent of highly religious respondents agree that all Muslim Americans should register their whereabouts with the government and that Muslim civic and volunteer organizations should be infiltrated. In contrast, fewer than half as many respondents with low religiosity feel the same way. Roughly one third of moderately religious respondents agree that Muslim Americans should register their whereabouts, that mosques should be closely surveilled, and that Muslim civic organizations should be infiltrated.

In 2005 the Pew Research Center asked the American public their impressions of Muslim Americans and 55 percent answered that they were favorable, 25 percent answered that they were unfavorable, and 20 percent had no opinion.

The chart in Table 3.5 compares opinions of Muslim Americans against a range of demographic characteristics.

Blacks, persons under thirty years of age, college graduates, persons with family annual incomes of more than $75,000, and liberal democrats hold the most favorable views toward American Muslims.

When Muslim Americans are compared against Catholics, Jews, Evangelical Christians, and Atheists, concerning respondents favorable views, Jews and Catholics come out with a much higher percentage of favorable opinions. Muslim Americans and Evangelical Christians receive lower and similar favorable views and atheists receive the lowest percentage of favorable opinions.

In July 2006 Gallup conducted a national survey that asked: "Do you think Muslims living in the United States are loyal to the United States?" to which 49 percent answered "yes" and 39 percent answered "no."

In response to an item that asked whether Muslim Americans were sympathetic to the Al-Qaeda terrorist organization 34 percent answered "yes" and 50 percent "no."

Shown in Table 3.7 are a series of items about Americans' perceptions and feelings about Muslim Americans.

A large majority of Americans believe American Muslims are committed to their religious beliefs but less than half believe they are respectful of other religions and only about a third believe they are respectful of women.

Over half (59 percent) of the respondents would not be in favor of requiring Muslim Americans to carry a special ID card or to undergo more intensive security checks at airports (59 percent). And finally 59 percent responded "no" when asked "If you honestly assessed yourself would you say that you have at least some feelings of prejudice against Muslims or not?"

Table 3.6
Favorable and Unfavorable Opinions, Muslim Americans
Compared with Catholics, Jews, Evangelical Christians and Atheists

----Favorable---   ---Unfavorable---

		Total	Very	Mostly	Total	Very	Mostly	(VOL.) Never Heard of	(VOL.) Can't Rate/Ref
a.F1	Catholics	73	24	49	14	4	10	0	13=100
	Mid-July, 2003	69	21	48	18	6	12	*	13=100
	March, 2002	74	19	55	13	4	9	*	13=100
	Mid-Nov.,2001	78	29	49	8	3	5	*	14=100
	March, 2001	74	19	55	13	3	10	1	12=100
	September, 2000 (RVs)	78	29	49	9	3	6	*	13=100
b.F1	Jews	77	23	54	7	2	5	*	16=100
	Late May, 2005	77	37	40	7	2	5	--	16=100
	Mid-July, 2003	72	20	52	9	3	6	1	18=100
	March, 2002	74	18	56	9	2	7	*	17=100
	Mid-Nov., 2001	75	24	51	7	2	5	*	18=100
	March, 2001	72	16	56	10	2	8	*	18=100
	September, 2000 (RVs)	77	27	50	8	3	5	*	15=100
	June, 1997	82	26	56	9	2	7	1	8=100
c.F1	Evangelical Christians	57	17	40	19	5	14	5	19=100
	Mid-July, 2003	58	18	40	18	6	12	3	21=100
	March, 2002	55	13	42	18	5	13	7	20=100
	March, 2001	55	13	42	16	4	12	8	21=100
	September, 2000 (RVs)	63	21	42	16	3	13	3	18=100
	February, 1996	39	13	26	38	15	23	11	12=100
	July, 1994	43	10	33	32	10	22	11	14=100
	May, 1990	43	12	31	38	19	19	7	12=100
d.F1	Muslim Americans	55	9	46	25	9	16	*	20=100
	Mid-July, 2003	51	10	41	24	9	15	1	24=100
	March, 2002	54	8	46	22	8	14	2	22=100
	Mid-Nov., 2001	59	15	44	17	5	12	1	23=100
	March, 2001	45	7	38	24	8	16	4	27=100
	September, 2000 (RVs)	50	11	39	21	8	13	2	27=100
e.F1	Atheists, that is, people who don't believe in God	35	7	28	50	28	22	0	15=100
	Mid-July 2003	34	7	27	52	33	19	*	14=100
	March, 2002	34	5	29	54	31	23	*	12=100
	Mid-November 2001	32	7	25	49	28	21	*	19=100

Table 3.7
Muslim Americans Are:

	Responses (percent)
Committed to their religious beliefs:	
Applies	87
Does not apply	7
Respectful of other religions	
Applies	47
Does not apply	40
Too extreme in their religious beliefs	
Applies	44
Does not apply	46
Respectful of women	
Applies	35
Does not apply	52

In 2007, a series of questions were asked on national surveys conducted in Great Britain, France, Italy, Spain, Germany, and the United States on attitudes toward the Muslim community in each of the countries.

At 58 percent, the United States joined France and Germany in not believing Muslim Americans pose a threat to national security. At 47 percent, they joined France and Italy in believing that Muslim Americans have become the subject of unjustified criticism or prejudice. Only 34 percent of the Spanish public and 39 percent of the British public share that view. Less than 10 percent of the publics in any of the countries believe their Muslim community has little power. At 46 percent the British public has the highest percentage who believe Muslims have too much power, more than half of the percentage of the American public (20 percent).

At 40, 39, and 36 percent more American, German, and British respondents than respondents in the other countries said they would object if their child wanted to marry a Muslim. At 28 percent, Americans joined the Spanish in having the smallest percentage who said they have friends who are Muslims. All in all, the Americans' opinions were less hostile or negative than the British and less friendly and positive than the French, each of which were the two outliers.

Table 3.8
Muslims as Threat to National Security

	Great Britain %	France %	Italy %	Spain %	Germany %	United States %
Unweighted base	1,111	1,029	1,056	1,061	1,086	1,055
Yes, the presence of Muslims presents a threat	38	20	30	23	28	21
No, the presence of Muslims does not present a threat	45	68	56	45	58	58
Not Sure	17	11	14	32	14	21

Note: Percentages may not add up to 100% due to rounding.
Source: Harris Interactive Polls (Table 1) *http://www.businesswire.com/portal/site/ google/index.jsp?ndmViewId=news_view&newsI*...accessed 9/9/2008.

Table 3.9
"Have Muslims in Your Country Become the
Subject of Unjustified Criticism and Prejudice or Not?"

	Great Britain %	France %	Italy %	Spain %	Germany %	United States %
Unweighted base	1,111	1,029	1,056	1,061	1,086	1,055
Yes	39	51	49	34	40	47
No	44	30	38	47	43	30
Not sure	17	19	13	19	17	23

Note: Percentages may not add up to 100% due to rounding.

The last survey also conducted in 2007 compared American public opinion toward the Muslim community against Jews, Catholics, Evangelical Christians, Mormons, and atheists. We found that about half of the public held favorable views of American Muslims and Mormons compared to three quarters who reported holding favorable views toward Jews and Catholics. Atheists were perceived favorably by only a third of the American public.

Table 3.10
"Do You Think Muslims Have Too Much, Too Little or the
Right Amount of Political Power in Your Country?"

	Great Britain %	France %	Italy %	Spain %	Germany %	United States %
Unweighted base	1,111	1,029	1,056	1,061	1,086	1,055
Too little	7	8	4	6	3	8
Too much	46	19	34	23	33	20
The right amount	19	41	26	36	37	23
Not sure	28	32	35	35	27	49

Note: Percentages may not add up to 100% due to rounding.

Table 3.11
"Would You Object if Your Child Wanted to Marry a Muslim?

	Great Britain %	France %	Italy %	Spain %	Germany %	United States %
Unweighted base	492	484	426	453	571	493
Yes	36	19	29	20	39	40
No	41	51	46	50	38	31
Not sure	23	30	25	30	22	29

Note: Percentages may not add up to 100% due to rounding.

Table 3.12
"Do You Have Any Friends Who Are Muslim?"

	Great Britain %	France %	Italy %	Spain %	Germany %	United States %
Unweighted base	1,111	1,029	1,056	1,061	1,086	1,055
Yes	38	69	32	27	37	28
No	55	28	67	70	61	60
Not sure	7	3	2	3	2	12

Note: Percentages may not add up to 100% due to rounding.

Table 3.13
American Public Opinion toward Muslim Community, against Jews, Catholics, Evangelical Christians, Mormons, and Atheists.

Group	Percent Favorable
Jews	76
Catholics	76
Evangelical Christians	60
Mormons	53
Muslim Americans	53
Atheists	35

Note

1. Abdul Malik Mujahid, *Muslims in America: Profile.* Monthly Impact International, London, UK: December 2000. On *http://www.allied-media.com/AM/AM-profile*, accessed 9/15/08.

4

Public Opinion toward Gays and Lesbians

The rights of gay and lesbian citizens in the United States has been a salient issue in recent years, seen through both the amount of legislation addressing the issue and its presence on presidential candidates' platforms. Many changes in laws and policies have happened only in recent years. For example, in 1973, the American Psychiatric Association removed homosexuality from its list of mental disorders.[1] Many advocacy groups and politicians have attempted to change federal laws regarding the legal rights of same-sex couples. In 2006, a proposal for a constitutional amendment banning gay marriage was rejected by the U.S. Congress.[2] In 1996, the Defense of Marriage Act (DOMA) was passed, which allows states the freedom to choose if they will recognize same-sex marriages from other states. DOMA also defines "marriage" and "spouse" in Federal law; marriage being the legal union of a man and woman and a spouse being the husband or wife of the opposite sex.[3] Some argue that the Act violates the full faith and credit clause of the Constitution that requires each state to honor the laws of other states.[4]

Many states afford gay and lesbian citizens different rights. In 1962, Illinois became the first state to decriminalize homosexual acts between consenting adults in private.[5] In 1982, Wisconsin became the first state to outlaw discrimination on the basis of sexual orientation.[6] In 2000, Vermont became the first state to legally recognize same-sex civil unions. Connecticut followed in 2005 and New Jersey in 2006.[7] In 2004, Massachusetts began issuing marriage licenses to same-sex couples as a result of the court's ruling that barring gays and lesbians from marrying violates the state constitution.[8] In 2008, a New York State appeals court voted that valid same-sex marriages performed in other states must be recognized by employers in New York, granting same-sex couples the same rights as other couples.[9] Also in 2008, Oregon passed a law that allows same-sex couples to register as domestic partners, granting them the same spousal rights as married couples. The California Supreme Court also ruled in 2008 that same-sex couples have a constitutional right to marry.[10] California began issuing marriage licenses to same-sex couples in June 2008. Although California and Massachusetts are the only states that allow same-sex couples to marry, Rhode Island recognizes same-sex marriages from other states.[11] In addition, Connecticut, Vermont, New Jersey, and New Hampshire provide for civil unions and Hawaii, Maine, the District of Columbia, Washington State, and Oregon provide rights to same-sex couples through domestic partnerships.[12]

There have been many recent U.S. Supreme Court cases addressing the rights of gays and lesbians. The 1986 case of *Bowers v. Hardwick* held that gays do not have a fundamental right to engage in sodomy.[13] In the 1998 case of *Oncale v. Sundowner Offshore Services, Inc.,* the U.S. Supreme Court held that sexual harassment by persons of one sex against persons of the same sex is actionable under Title VII.[14] In the 2000 case of *Boy Scouts of America v. Dale,* the U.S. Supreme Court ruled that a New Jersey anti-discrimination law that required the Boy Scouts of America to admit an openly gay man as a scoutmaster violated the Boy Scouts' first amendment right of expressive association.[15] In 2003, the Supreme Court ruled in *Lawrence v. Texas* that a Texas law that prohibited sexual acts between same-sex couples was unconstitutional. The Court held that the right to privacy protects the right for adults to engage in private, consensual homosexual activity and overruled *Bowers v. Hardwick.*[16]

Although most states and the federal government do not have laws prohibiting discrimination based on sexual orientation, in 1998 President Clinton issued an executive order prohibiting such discrimination in federal civilian employment.[17] In 2003, the U.S. Circuit Court of Appeals in San Francisco ruled that schools failing to protect gay students from harassment could be in violation of federal law.[18] The court held that a school must take steps to eliminate harassment when it learns that lesbian, gay and bisexual students are abused at school.[19] All but five states—Arkansas, Georgia, Indiana, South Carolina, and Wyoming—have hate crime laws based on sexual orientation or gender identity.[20]

Gays and lesbians, especially same-sex partners, are often not treated in the same manner as opposite-sex couples. For tax purposes, gay and lesbian couples must file individually even if their incomes are combined. Same-sex couples are therefore taxed more heavily than married couples who are taxed jointly.[21] In 2005, the George W. Bush administration rewrote the rules governing the adjudication of security clearances.

Previous language stated that a person's sexual orientation "may not be used as a basis for or a disqualifying factor in determining a person's eligibility for a security clearance." The language was rewritten to say that security clearances cannot be denied "solely on the basis of sexual orientation of the individual."[22] In 2002, President Bush signed legislation allowing death benefits of public safety officers killed on September 11, 2001 to go to a beneficiary other than an immediate family member. This is believed to be the first time federal benefits have been available to survivors in gay partnerships.[23]

The United States currently does not give same-sex couples benefits in terms of immigration. The Uniting American Families Act, first introduced in 2000, would let U.S. citizens and permanent residents sponsor their foreign-born partners applying for U.S. citizenship.[24] The bill has been reintroduced in Congressional sessions several times after having failed to pass. In August 2008, the bill picked up its 100th Congressional co-sponsor. If it fails to pass in the 2008 session, it will be reintroduced in 2009.[25] The United States does grant asylum to gays and lesbians from other countries who are persecuted for their sexual orientation.[26]

The military currently operates under a policy known as "Don't Ask, Don't Tell." This policy permits gays and lesbians to serve in the military provided they do not disclose their sexual orientation.[27] Additionally, military personnel are not permitted to inquire about a service member's sexual orientation. The law enacting this policy was passed in 1993 and has come under scrutiny by many civil rights groups. President Clinton intended to completely revoke the prohibition against gays and lesbians serving in the military but was met with strong opposition by many conservative and religious groups.[28]

Many people allege that the policy limits the enlistment of qualified people and requires the discharge of highly trained personnel who have publicly acknowledged their sexual orientation.[29] Since the policy took effect in 1994, more than 12,000 personnel have been discharged under it.[30] It has been estimated to cost the military $218 million to recruit and train replacements for those discharged under the policy.[31] Supporters of the policy allege that allowing gays and lesbians to serve openly in the military would drive away more people than would be discharged under the policy.[32] In July 2008, lawmakers held congressional hearings reexamining the policy for the first time since it came into law.[33]

The following section reports national poll data on gays and lesbians.

National Poll Data

The first time attitudes toward homosexuality appeared on a national poll was June 1977. The question asked was:

Do you think homosexual relations between consenting adults should be or should not be legal?

In 1977, 43 percent answered "should be legal," 43 percent said "should not be legal," and 14 percent said they had no opinion.

Between June 1977 and May 2008, the responses to that question are shown in the table below.

Table 4.1
Do You Think Homosexual Relations between
Consenting Adults Should Be or Should Not Be Legal?

Date	Should be Legal %	Should not be Legal %	No Opinion %
2008 May 8-11	55	40	5
2007 May 10-13	59	37	4
2006 May 8-11^	56	40	4
2005 Aug 22-25	49	44	7
2005 May 2-5	52	43	5
2004 May 2-4	52	43	5
2004 Jan 9-11	46	49	5
2003 Jul 25-27	48	46	6
2003 Jul 18-20	50	44	6
2003 May 19-21	59	37	4
2003 May 5-7	60	35	5
2002 May 6-9	52	43	5
2001 May 10-14	54	42	4
1999 Feb 8-9	50	43	7
1996 Nov 21-24	44	47	9
1992 Jun 4-8	48	44	8
1989 Oct 12-15	47	36	17
1988 Jul 1-7	35	57	11
1987 Mar 14-18	33	55	12
1986 Sep 13-17	33	54	13
1986 Jul 11-14	32	57	11
1985 Nov 11-18	44	47	9
1982 Jun 25-28	45	39	16
1977 Jun 17-20	43	43	14

^Asked of half sample.

At 32 and 33 percent, 1986 and 1987 marked the years in which the lowest percentage of respondents believed that homosexual relations between consenting adults should be legal. At 60 percent, 2003 marked the year in which the highest percentage thought homosexual relations should be legal. From May 2006 through May 2008, between 55 and 59 percent of the respondents thought homosexual relations should be legal.

From 1982 through 2008, the American public was asked:

Do you feel that homosexuality should be considered an acceptable alternative lifestyle or not?

When the question was first posed in 1982 only 34 percent answered that homosexuality should be considered an acceptable alternative lifestyle. By 2008, 57 percent said they believed it should be an acceptable lifestyle.

Table 4.2
Do You Feel That Homosexuality Should Be
Considered an Acceptable Alternative Lifestyle or Not?

Date	Acceptable %	Not Acceptable %	No Opinion %
2008 May 8-11	57	40	3
2007 Sep 7-8	48	46	6
2007 May 10-13	57	39	3
2006 May 8-11^	54	41	4
2005 May 2-5^	51	45	4
2004 May 2-4	54	42	4
2003 Jul 25-27	46	49	5
2003 May 5-7	54	43	3
2002 May 6-9	51	44	5
2001 May 10-14	52	43	5
1999 Feb 8-9^	50	46	4
1997 Apr 18-20^	42	52	6
1996 Mar 15-17^	44	50	6
1992 Jun 4-8	38	57	5
1982 Jun 25-28	34	51	15

^Asked of half sample.

When asked, between June 1977 and May 2008,

As you may know, there has been considerable discussion in the news regarding the rights of homosexual men and women. In general, do you think homosexuals should or should not have equal rights in terms of job opportunities?

The respondents answering "yes" ranged from 56 percent in 1977 to 89 percent in 2006, 2007, and 2008.

Over the same time period, 1977 through 2008, the public was asked:

In your view is homosexuality something a person is born with or is homosexuality due to factors such as upbringing and environment?

In 1977, 13 percent of the respondents said that homosexuality is something that a person is born with and 14 percent said that homosexu-

Table 4.3
As You May Know, There Has Been Considerable Discussion in the News Regarding the Rights of Homosexual Men and Women.
In General, Do You Think Homosexuals Should or Should Not Have Equal Rights in Terms of Job Opportunities?

Date	Yes, should %	No, should not %	Depends (vol.) %	No Opinion %
2008 May 8-11	89	8	1	1
2007 May 10-13	89	8	1	2
2006 May 8-11	89	9	1	1
2005 May 2-5	87	11	1	1
2004 May 2-4	89	8	1	2
2003 May 19-21	88	10	1	1
2003 May 5-7	88	9	2	1
2002 May 6-9	86	11	1	2
2001 May 10-14	85	11	3	1
1999 Feb 8-9	83	13	2	2
1996 Nov 21-24	84	12	2	2
1993 Apr 22-24	80	14	--	6
1992 Jun 4-7	74	18	--	8
1989 Oct 12-15	71	18	--	11
1982 Jun 25-28	59	28	--	13
1977 Jun 17-20	56	33	--	11

(vol.) = Volunteered response.

Table 4.4
**In Your View Is Homosexuality Something a Person Is Born with or Is
Homosexuality Due to Factors Such as Upbringing and Environment?**

Date	Born with %	Upbringing/ Environment %	Both (vol.) %	Neither (vol.) %	No Opinion %
2008 May 8-11	41	38	9	2	9
2007 May 10-13	42	35	11	2	9
2006 May 8-11^	42	37	11	2	8
2005 May 2-5	38	44	10	2	6
2004 May 2-4	37	41	11	3	8
2003 May 5-7	38	44	11	2	5
2002 May 6-9	40	36	12	4	8
2001 May 10-14	40	39	9	3	9
1999 Feb 8-9	34	44	13	1	8
1996 Nov 21-24	31	40	13	3	13
1989 Oct 12-15	19	48	12	2	19
1982 Jun 25-28	17	52	13	2	16
1977 Jun 17-20	13	56	14	3	15

(vol.)=Volunteered response.
^Asked of half sample.

ality is both something a person is born with and due to factors such as
upbringing and environment. By 2008, 41 and 9 percent, respectively,
answered "born with" and "both."

From March 1996 through May 2008, the public was asked:

Do you think marriages between same-sex couples should or should not be recognized
by the law as valid, with the same rights as traditional marriages?

The responses in Table 4.5 show that a majority of the American
public does not believe that marriages between same-sex couples should
be recognized as legally valid. In 1996, over two thirds did not believe
same sex marriages should be recognized as legally valid and 56 percent
in 2008 did not believe so.

A related, but more strongly-worded question, was asked between
July 2003 and May 2008.

Table 4.5
Do You Think Marriages between Same-Sex couples Should or Should Not Be Recognized by the Law as Valid, with the Same Rights as Traditional Marriages?

Date	Should be valid %	Should not be valid %	No Opinion %
2008 May 8-11*	40	56	4
2007 May 10-13	46	53	1
2006 May 8-11*	42	56	2
2006 May 8-11^*	39	58	4
2005 Aug 22-25^	37	59	4
2004 May 2-4^	42	55	3
1999 Feb 8-9^	35	62	3
1996 Mar 15-17^	27	68	5

^WORDING: Do you think marriages between homosexuals should or should not be recognized by the law as valid, with the same rights as traditional marriages?

*Asked of a half sample.

Table 4.6
Would You Favor or Oppose a Constitutional Amendment That Would Define Marriage as Being between a Man and a Woman, Thus Barring Marriages between Gay or Lesbian Couples?

Date	Favor %	Oppose %	No Opinion %
2008 May 8-11^	49	48	3
2006 May 8-11	50	47	3
2005 Apr. 29-May 1	53	44	3
2005 Mar 18-20	57	37	6
2004 Jul 19-21^	48	46	6
2004 May 2-4	51	45	4
2004 Mar 5-7	50	45	5
2004 Feb 9-12	53	44	3
2004 Feb 6-8^	47	47	6
2003 Jul 18-20	50	45	5

^Asked of a half sample.

While slightly fewer than the 56 percent who answered that they did not believe marriages between same-sex couples should be legally valid, in 2008 almost half, 49 percent, said they would favor a constitutional amendment that would bar marriages between gay and lesbian couples.

Between October 2000 and May 2004, the following item appeared on national polls:

> Would you favor or oppose a law that would allow homosexual couples to legally form civil unions, giving them some of the legal rights of married couples?

The responses were divided almost evenly, 49 and 48 percent, between those who favored civil unions and those opposed to them. Note that in 2004 when respondents were asked whether marriages between same-sex couples should or should not be recognized as legally valid 42 percent answered they should be valid. The public views civil unions slightly more favorably.

Table 4.7
**Would You Favor or Oppose a Law That Would Allow
Homosexual Couples to Legally Form Civil Unions, Giving
Them Some of the Legal Rights of Married Couples?**

Date	Favor %	Oppose %	No Opinion %
2004 May 2-4	49	48	3
2003 Jul 25-27	40	57	3
2003 May 5-7	49	49	2
2002 May 6-9	46	51	3
2002 Apr 8-11	45	46	9
2002 Feb 8-10	41	53	6
2001 May 10-14	44	52	4
2000 Oct 25-28^	42	54	4

^WORDING: Suppose that on election day this year you could vote on key issues as well as candidates. Please tell me whether you would vote for or against each one of the following propositions. Would you vote—[RANDOM ORDER]? (For or against a law that would allow homosexual couples to legally form civil unions, giving them some of the legal rights of married couples.)

Concerning service in the military, the public was asked in January 2000 and again in July 2007:

> As you may know, under the current military policy, no one in the military is asked whether or not they are gay. But if they reveal that they are gay or they engage in homosexual activity, they will be discharged from the military. Do you personally think gays should be allowed to serve openly in the military, gays should be allowed to serve under the current policy, or gays should not be allowed to serve in the military under any circumstances?

Those who favored allowing gays to serve openly in the military increased from 41 percent to 46 percent.

In 1999 and 2006, the American public was asked whether they favored or opposed allowing gays and lesbians to adopt children. In 1999, 38 percent said they favored and in 2006, 46 percent answered that they favored allowing gays and lesbians to adopt. Women at 43 and 50 percent in 1999 and 2006 favored it as opposed to men at 33 and 41 percent. Younger respondents (ages 18-29, compared to those over 30) and more educated respondents (college graduates) favored allowing gays and lesbians to adopt.

Finally, when asked whether they would like to see homosexuality more widely accepted, the responses indicate a slight increase among

Table 4.8
As You May Know, under the Current Military Policy, No One in the Military is Asked whether or Not They Are Gay. But if They Reveal That They Are Gay or They Engage in Homosexual Activity, They Will Be Discharged from the Military. Do You Personally Think Gays Should Be Allowed to Serve Openly in the Military, Gays Should Be Allowed to Serve under the Current Policy, or Gays Should Not Be Allowed to Serve in the Military under Any Circumstances?

Date	Serve Openly %	Serve under current policy %	Not serve under any circumstances %	No Opinion %
2007 Jul 6-8	46	36	15	3
2000 Jan 13-16^	41	38	17	4

^WORDING: As you may know, under the current military policy, no one in the military is asked whether or not they are homosexual. But if they reveal that they are homosexual and they engage in homosexual activity, they will be discharged from the military. Do you personally think—gays should be allowed to serve openly in the military, gays should be allowed to serve under the current policy, or gays should not be allowed to serve in the military under any circumstances?

Table 4.9
Would You Like to See Homosexuality Be More Widely
Accepted in This Nation, Less Widely Accepted, or Is the
Acceptance of Homosexuality in This Nation Today about Right?

Date	More Widely Accepted %	Less Widely Accepted %	About Right %	Other (vol.) %	No Opinion %
2008 Jan 4-6	34	32	28	1	5
2007 Jan 15-18	33	37	27	*	3
2006 Jan 9-12	31	38	27	1	3
2005 Jan 3-5	29	36	30	1	4
2004 Jan 12-15	30	35	31	1	3
2003 Jan 13-16	28	31	34	1	6
2002 Jan 7-9	29	33	32	1	5
2001 Jan 10-14	29	34	33	1	3

*Less than 0.5 percent.
(vol.)=Volunteered response.

those who desire greater acceptance from 29 percent in January 2001 to 34 percent in January 2008. The percent of respondents who believe that acceptance of homosexuality is about right decreased from 33 to 28 percent. In sum, almost two thirds of the American public (62 percent) would like to see homosexuality more widely accepted or believe it is about right as of 2008.

We conclude with the view that attitudes toward gays and lesbians on almost all of the issues posed over the past thirty plus years have shown more positive and accepting attitudes, although American society remains generally divided as of the present.

Notes

1.   Infoplease, "The American Gay Rights Movement: A Timeline" available at: *http://www.infoplease.com/ipa/A0761909.html* (August 07, 2008).
2.   Library of Congress, available at: *http://thomas.loc.gov/cgi-bin/bdquery/z?d108:SJ00030:@@@L&summ2=m&* (August 10, 2008).
3.   Lectric Law Library, "Defense of Marriage Act," available at: *http://www.lectlaw.com/files/leg23.htm* (August 10, 2008).
4.   Gay Law Net, available at: *http://www.gaylawnet.com/* (August 05, 2008).
5.   Infoplease, "The American Gay Rights Movement: A Timeline," available at: *http://www.infoplease.com/ipa/A0761909.html* (August 07, 2008).

6.   *Ibid.*
7.   *Ibid.*
8.   *Ibid.*
9.   *Ibid.*
10. *Ibid.*
11. National Conference of State Legislatures, "Same Sex Marriage," available at: *http://www.ncslorg/programs/cyf/samesex.htm* (August 12, 2008).
12. *Ibid.*
13. Legal Information Institute, available at: *http://www.law.cornell.edu/supct/html/historics/USSC_CR_0478_0186_ZS.html* (August 10, 2008).
14. The U.S. Equal Employment Opportunity Commission, available at: *http://www.eeoc.gov/federal/digest/xi-5-2.html* (August 10, 2008).
15. Boy Scouts of America v. Dale, available at: *http://law.jrank.org/pages/4831/Boy-Scouts-America-v-Dale.html* (August 10, 2008).
16. Duke Law, "Lawrence v. Texas," available at: *http://www.law.duke.edu/publiclaw/supremecourtonline/commentary/lawvtex.html* (August 10, 2008).
17. Gay Law Net, available at: *http://www.gaylawnet.com/* (August 05, 2008).
18. *Ibid.*
19. ACLU of Northern California, "Federal Appeals Court Says Schools Must Protect Gay Students from Harassment," available at: *http://www.aclunc.org/news/press_releases/federal_appeals_court_says_schools_must_protect_gay_students_from_harassment.shtml* (August 11, 2008).
20. National Gay and Lesbian Taskforce, available at: *http://www.thetaskforce.org/downloads/reports/issue_maps/hate_crimes_04_08_color.pdf* (August 5, 2008).
21. Gay Law Net, available at: *http://www.gaylawnet.com/* (August 05, 2008).
22. *Ibid.*
23. *Ibid.*
24. Human Rights Watch, "The Uniting American Families Act," available at: *http://www.hrw.org/campaigns/lgbt/uaf_act.htm* (August 08, 2008).
25. San Francisco Bay Area Independent Media Center, "Uniting American Families Act (UAFA) Gets 100th House Co-Sponsor," available at: *http://www.indybay.org/newsitems/2008/08/03/18522577.php* (August 11, 2008).
26. National Public Radio, "Gay Refugees Seek Asylum in U.S.," available at: *http://www.npr.org/templates/story/story.php?storyId=12734276* (August 12, 2008).
27. Los Angeles Times, "Don't Ask, Don't Tell" policy is reexamined," available at: *http://www.latimes.com/news/printedition/asection/la-na-dontask24-2008jul24,0,15454633.story* (August 10, 2008).
28. Infoplease, "The American Gay Rights Movement: A Timeline," available at: *http://www.infoplease.com/ipa/A0761909.html* (August 07, 2008).
29. Human Rights Watch, "Uniform Discrimination: The 'Don't Ask, Don't Tell' Policy of the U.S. Military," available at: *http://www.hrw.org/reports/2003/usa0103/* (August 02, 2008).
30. *Ibid.*
31. *Ibid.*
32. *Ibid.*
33. *Newsweek*, "Beginning the Conversation," available at: *http://www.newsweek.com/id/147961* (August 12, 2008).

5

Public Opinion toward Immigrants

One of the miracles of this country is that so many people from all over the world came and settled here. Between 1810 and the present time, over 40,000,000 immigrants came and remained in the United States. They came mostly in the past 110 years, but even from 1810 (the earliest date for which we have official statistics) to 1880 some 10 million immigrants arrived and remained.

From the beginning until 1960, the large majority—over 80 percent—came from Europe; in the early period mostly from Ireland, Britain, and Germany. After the 1880s, the movement shifted eastward and the largest groups of immigrants came from Italy, Austria-Hungary, and Russia. After the end of the First World War there was another shift, instigated by some rather stringent pieces of legislation (which we shall discuss later), and many of the immigrants came from the Western Hemisphere countries. After 1960, European immigration declined to 26 percent; and Western Hemisphere countries, primarily Mexico, Cuba, and Canada, comprised almost 50 percent of U.S. immigration. In the 1970s and 1980s, Asian immigration, mostly from the Philippines, Vietnam and, Korea, increased dramatically and accounted for about one third of the total U.S. immigration. Thus far, the rest of the world, Africa, Australia, and New Zealand, accounts for less than 3 percent.

Before the Revolution, almost all of the colonies had laws that kept out some groups. All of the New England colonies except Rhode Island excluded non-puritans. In 1666, Maryland passed the first naturalization act in the colonies and in doing so limited the privilege of citizenship to foreign-born Protestants. In 1671, Virginia, and in 1696 South Carolina, adopted similar legislation. During the French and Indian wars in 1689, Huguenot communities in New York, Pennsylvania, Virginia, and Rhode Island were attacked because the Huguenots were suspected of loyalty to the French. German settlers were attacked in Pennsylvania in the 1750s. All of the colonies passed laws against voting and office holding for Catholics and Jews. They worried about the prospect of immigrants becoming public charges. In 1700, Rhode Island demanded a bond of 50 pounds from each vessel master carrying foreigners to insure that aliens likely to become dependent on public aid would not be brought into the colony.

Almost a hundred years later, the situation had changed and the colonies were angered at Britain's acts to disrupt immigration by placing heavy duties. In 1774, the British government ended immigration to the colonies on grounds that the influx of newcomers would strengthen the growing calls for independence. Thus, among the charges made against the King stated in the Declaration of Independence were that he was attempting to keep the colonies depopulated, that he refused to recognize naturalization acts passed by colonial assemblies, and that he restricted westward settlements.

At the Philadelphia Convention that drafted the Constitution in 1787, immigration was not one of the major topics for debate. But the issue did come up and several matters were resolved. It is interesting that at the time of the Constitutional Convention sharp lines were not drawn between Federalists and Republicans on the pros and cons of immigration and the status and rights of the foreign-born. Less than ten years later, the Federalists became the opponents of and the Republicans the supporters of immigration and the rights of the foreign-born. But Alexander Hamilton, a leading Federalist (who was born in the West Indies), argued that "immigrants could make important contributions to the welfare of the nation and that they should be regarded as on the level of the first citizens." James Madison claimed, "that part of America which has encouraged the foreigners most has advanced the most rapidly in population, agriculture and the arts." John Adams, under whose administration the Alien and Sedition laws were passed, stated: "It is our business to render our country an asylum to receive all who may fly to it." But Pierce Butler of South Carolina and Gouverneur Morris of Pennsylvania feared that immigrants would retain the political principles of the despotic countries they left behind.

In the end, the only restrictions placed on the foreign-born were that they were not eligible for the Presidency, and that Senators had to be citizens for nine years and Representatives for seven years. In 1790, Congress passed the first federal law defining a uniform rule for the naturalization of aliens: any free white male or female who resided for two years within the limits and under the jurisdiction of the United States could acquire American citizenship. The law also read "the review of naturalization applications was to be made by any common law court of records in any one of the States."

Authority over immigrants continued to be exercised mainly by state governments and local officials until after the Civil War. The Federal Government kept no records of immigration until 1820. Not until 1850 did the U.S. Census distinguish between foreign and native born. In 1864, Congress established a "Bureau of Immigration."

But to return to the last decade of the eighteenth century, by the mid-1790s the Federalists were sufficiently concerned by the types of foreigners who were coming to American shores (Englishmen sympathetic to the French Revolution who found life in England intolerable, Irish who fled after the unsuccessful rebellion of 1798) that in 1795 they lengthened the term of residence for naturalization to five years, and then, in 1798 (in the form of the Aliens Act) to fourteen years; insisting also that aliens must make a declaration of intention five years before obtaining their final papers. The passage of the Alien and Sedition Acts also gave the President, John Adams, the authority to deport undesirable foreigners. After the Republican-Democrats gained power in 1801 with the election of Thomas Jefferson, the fourteen years requirement was repealed and replaced by five years. It has remained that down to the present.

American historian, Marcus Hansen, characterized the freedom that immigrants sought as mostly freedom from laws and customs that curbed individual economic enterprise. In the cities of Europe, they wanted to escape regulations of guild and trade unions; in the country, they sought exemption from traditional restrictions upon the transfer of land and the conduct of agriculture. They wanted, in essence, the freedom to buy, sell, bargain, to work or loaf, to become rich or poor.

Between 1830 and 1860 more immigrants came from Ireland than any other country. The first widespread manifestation of anti-Catholic, anti-foreign sentiment occurred in the 1830s. Although as early as 1806, on Christmas Day a riot broke out in New York City between mobs of nativists and Irishmen in which many people were hurt and houses were looted.

Anti-Catholic, anti-immigrant sentiments coalesced into political parties bearing such names as the "Native American Party" (1840s), and the most famous of all, the "Know Nothing Party" (1850s). Supporters of these parties rioted in the port cities, they burned Catholic churches, they sought to extend the naturalization requirement to twenty-one years and to exclude Catholics and all foreign-born from holding public office. The leaders of the Know Nothing Party developed the slogan, "Whose country is this, anyway?" They claimed that the foreigners were degrading American character and morals.

Following the Civil War, the "Know Nothing" movement all but disappeared and the number of immigrants arriving in the United States kept getting larger and larger. By the 1870s the term "new immigrants" was widely used to refer to persons arriving from Southern and Eastern Europe. The phrase "new immigrants' referred not only to their countries of origin, which differed from those of the earlier cohorts, but to the types of people they were. For example, they were more likely to be Catholics than Protestants, they were not English speaking, they were, in the majority, not skilled craftsmen or farm owners. Physically they had characteristics that set them apart from the natives more than the earlier cohorts of immigrants; and also more than the earlier cohorts, they were city dwellers. They crowded together in the cities closest to the ports from which they entered.

While the "Know Nothing" movement receded into the background, other groups, movements, and political parties expressed consternation, anxiety, fear, and other negative reactions at the seemingly endless stream of new immigrants who kept arriving at America's doorstep. The major fears were that these "new types" would alter the quality of life in the United States, would lower the wage levels and standard of living of the U.S. worker, would increase the crime, illiteracy, and pauperism rates, and would lower the level of culture. They would overcrowd U.S. cities and make them dirty, ugly and dangerous, and they would fragment American values and loyalties.

Historians have characterized the period from 1880 to 1970 as the restrictionist era in U.S. immigration policy. It represented the first time that the Federal Government assumed an active and major role in determining immigration policy.

The first major piece of anti-immigrant legislation was the Chinese Exclusion Act of 1882, which suspended entry of Chinese workers for ten years and barred all foreign-born Chinese from acquiring citizenship. It marked the first time in U.S. history that a group of people was excluded because of their national characteristics.

Following the end of World War I, the Johnson Act, known as the Quota Act or the Immigration Act of 1921, introduced the system of national quotas. It was determined as the percentage of the number of immigrants from the country in question at a designated census. The 1921 Act limited the annual number of entrants of each admissible nationality to 3 percent of the foreign born of that nationality as recorded in the U.S. Census of 1910. It also set a limit on European immigration at 350,000. The 1921 Act had been vetoed earlier by President Woodrow Wilson. When Warren Harding took office, he signed it into law.

Quotas were established for countries in Europe, the Near East, Africa, Australia, and New Zealand. No quotas were imposed on immigrants from countries in the Western hemisphere.

In 1924, the year the 1921 Quota Act expired, Congress passed another National Quota Act, known for its cosponsors as the Johnson-Reed Act. This time it set national quotas at 2 percent of the 1890 population. The Quota Act of 1924 also provided that beginning July 1, 1927, the quota limit would be 150,000, allocated on the basis of the estimated national origins distribution of the population of continental United States in 1920. This portion of the 1924 Act was postponed twice. But it finally became effective on July 1, 1929. The Act barred from entry all aliens who were ineligible for citizenship.

In the first two decades of the twentieth century, Congress passed various other pieces of restrictionist legislation that limited groups on the basis of political activities and ideologies, and medical histories. Anarchists and epileptics, for example, were excluded by these measures.

The period between 1929 and 1939 saw little legislative action largely because there was so little immigration during those years. In 1932 immigration reached its lowest level since 1831. In fact, many more people were leaving than entering the United States. The worldwide depression was the major reason.

During the Second World War, in response to the labor shortage that the war created, Congress established the Bracero program, which permitted the entrance on a temporary basis of foreign agricultural laborers from Mexico, British Honduras, Barbados, and Jamaica. The Chinese Exclusion Law was repealed.

Immediately following the end of World War II, Congress passed a War Brides Act (1946), which admitted about 120,000 alien wives and children of U.S. servicemen on a non-quota basis. Two years later it passed a "Displaced Persons Act," which admitted 280,000 people over a two-year period. Regular immigration quotas were mortgaged at 50 percent each year for as many years as it would take to pay back the number of immigrants admitted under this act. In 1950, still retaining the mortgage principle, an additional 415,000 displaced persons were admitted over the next two-year period.

The Immigration and Nationality Act of 1952 sponsored by Senator Pat McCarran and Representative Francis Walter was the major piece of immigration legislation since the 1921 and 1924 Quota Acts. The McCarran-Walter Act changed the formula for the computation of annual quotas from any country to one sixth of 1 percent of the number of persons of national origin in the United States in 1920. It limited immigration from the eastern hemisphere to 150,000 per year. No ceilings were placed on western hemisphere immigration. The law removed racial barriers to immigration and naturalization. It established preferences for skilled workers and for relatives of U.S. citizens.

The Hungarian uprising in 1956 sparked the passage of the first of a series of Refugee Acts that have continued up to the present. In 1956 Congress allowed 21,000 Hungarian refugees to enter without regard for limitation quotas. In 1960, following the success of Fidel Castro in establishing a leftist regime in Cuba, the United States passed the Migration and Refugee Assistance Act, which facilitated the admission and resettlement of more than 600,000 Cuban refugees into the United States. In 1964 Congress ended the Bracero program it had inaugurated in 1942.

The Hart-Cellar Act of 1965 eliminated national origins as a basis for selection of immigrants to the United States. In its place it established an annual limit of 170,000 aliens who could enter the United States as immigrants and a per country quota of 20,000. Not included in the 170,000 figure were potential immigrants from western hemisphere countries. It set a ceiling of 120,000 on immigration from the western hemisphere, thus allowing for the admission of 290,000 immigrants per year. The Act established a system whereby immigration visas would be distributed according to a seven-point preference list that favored close relatives of U.S. citizens and those with needed occupational skills. Countries in the western hemisphere did not have a per country quota. The 1976 Immigration and Nationality Act extended the per country limitation of 20,000 to the western hemisphere. In 1978 the Act was amended to combine the ceiling for both the eastern and western hemispheres for a worldwide total of 290,000 immigrants per year.

The 1970s also witnessed the passage of legislation for the admission and resettlement of refugees, mainly from Southeast Asia, the Soviet Union, and Cuba. In 1975 the Indochinese Refugee Resettlement Program was enacted, allowing over 200,000 Indochinese refugees to enter. In one piece of legislation, the Refugee Act of 1980, the United States established an overall policy vis-à-vis the admission and resettlement of refugees to the United States. Refugees were defined in accordance with the UN Convention of 1951 as persons outside their homeland, unable or unwilling to return because of persecution or fear of persecution. The Act assumed a normal flow of 50,000 refugees per year. It permitted the president, in consultation with Congress, to increase the annual allocation. In 1980 the level was set at 230,000 admissions.

The Simpson-Mazoli Bill, passed in 1986, granted permanent resident status to aliens who lived continuously in the United States since January 1982 and established a system of sanctions against employers who knowingly hired illegals.

Four years later, the Immigration Act of 1990 was passed. That act, which allows some 675,000 immigrants to enter the United States per year, is a major example of the more open immigration policy that the U.S. has adopted.

National Poll Data

The basic question asked of the American public beginning in 1946 is shown in Table 5.1.

Note that at no time from 1946 to 2008 did more than 18 percent of the respondents favor increasing the number of immigrants allowed to enter the United States. We see that during periods of economic expansion and growth, during periods of recession and relatively high unemployment, during periods that included the Cold War and during periods marked by a relaxation of tension among the major powers, the American public's willingness to increase the number of immigrants ranged from 4 to 18 percent. And except for 1953 it is only in the twenty-first century that more than 10 percent favored the increase.

Between 2001 and 2008, the American public was asked:

On the whole, do you think immigration is a good thing or a bad thing for the country today?

The results in Table 5.2 show that in every year more than half of the respondents and in 2006, two thirds, answered that they believed it was a good thing.

When divided by ethnic background, white respondents' attitudes ranged from 51 to 68 percent; blacks from 46 to 60 percent and Hispanics from 65 to 76 percent.

The physical image that best describes the American public's attitude toward immigrants is that it sees them with rose-colored glasses turned backwards. In other words, those immigrants who came earlier, whenever "earlier" happens to be, are viewed as having made important and posi-

Table 5.1
Should U.S. Immigration Be Kept at Its Present Level, Increased, or Decreased?

---------- Response Categories ---------

Years	More/Increase	Same/Present Level	Fewer/Decrease	No Opinion/ Don't Know
1946[a]	5	32	37	12
1953	13	37	39	11
1965	8	39	33	20
1977	7	37	42	14
1981	5	22	65	8
1982	4	23	66	7
1986	7	35	49	9
1988	6	34	53	7
1990[b]	9	29	48	14
1992	4	29	54	13
1993	6	27	54	13
1995	7	24	65	4
1999	10	41	44	5
2000	13	41	38	8
2001	14	42	41	3
2002	17	26	54	3
2003	13	37	47	3
2004	14	33	49	4
2005	16	34	46	4
2006	17	42	39	2
2007	16	35	45	4
2008	18	39	39	3

Source: American Institute of Public Opinion (Storrs: Roper Center, University of Connecticut, 2000).
a) In 1946, the question was phrased: "Should we permit more persons from Europe to come to this country each year than we did before the war, should we keep the number about the same, or should we reduce the number?" "None" was offered as a choice and 14 percent selected it. In the subsequent polls, the question was usually phrased: "Should immigration be kept at its present level, increased, or decreased?"
b) In 1990, the question was phrased: "Is it your impression that the current immigration laws allow too many immigrants, too few immigrants, or about the right number of immigrants into this country every year?"

Table 5.2
"On the Whole, Do You Think Immigration Is a
Good Thing or a Bad Thing for the Country Today?"

Year	Good Thing %	Bad Thing %	Mixed %	No Opinion %
2001	62	31	5	2
2002	52	42	4	2
2003	58	36	4	2
2005	61	34	3	2
2006	67	28	4	1
2007	60	33	3	4
2008	64	30	4	2

Table 5.3
Public Opinion on Immigrants by Ethnicity, 1985-1993

	Benefit Country		Create Problems		Difference (Benefits-Problems)	
Nationality	1985	1993	1985	1993	1985	1993
Irish	78	76	5	11	73	65
Poles	72	65	7	15	65	50
Chinese	69	59	13	31	56	28
Koreans	52	53	23	33	29	20
Vietnamese	47	41	30	46	17	-5
Mexicans	44	29	37	59	7	-30
Haitians	31	19	35	65	-4	-46
Iranians	32	20	40	68	-12	-48
Cubans	29	24	55	64	-26	-40

Source: *USA Today/CNN*, 1993.

tive contributions to U.S. society, to its economy and culture. But those who seek entry now, whenever "now" happens to be, are viewed, at best, with ambivalence, and more likely with distrust and hostility.

In 1982, a national poll conducted by the Roper Center at the University of Connecticut said, "Since the beginning of our country people of many different religions, races, and nationalities have come here and settled. Here is a list of some different groups."

The question read: "Would you read down the list and, thinking both of what they have contributed to this country and have gotten from this country, for each one tell me whether you think, on balance, they have been a good thing or a bad thing for this country?"

We see in the responses shown in table 5.4 that in 1982, the immigrants from Southern and Eastern Europe (the Jews, Italians, and Poles) were viewed as having made positive contributions to U.S. society. The Chinese, against whom we passed special legislation (Chinese Exclusion Act, 1882) that barred all foreign-born Chinese from acquiring U.S. citizenship, were also viewed in a more positive than negative light. But the Koreans, Vietnamese, Haitians, and Cubans are perceived as bad for the United States.

In 1985 and 1993, a *USA Today/CNN* poll asked the American public whether the following nationalities have "benefitted the country" or "created problems." The results show that like the 1982 poll, the earlier

Table 5.4
"On the Whole Do You Think They Have Been a
Good Thing or a Bad Thing for This Country?"

Nationality	Good	Bad	Different in Percent(a)
English	66	6	60
Irish	62	7	55
Jews	59	9	50
Germans	57	11	46
Italians	56	10	46
Poles	53	12	41
Japanese	47	18	29
Chinese	44	19	25
Mexicans	25	4	21
Koreans	24	30	-6
Vietnamese	20	38	-18
Haitians	10	39	-29
Cubans	9	59	-50

Source: American Institute of Public Opinion (Storrs: Roper Center, University of Connecticut, 1982).
(a)The two categories not shown are "mixed feelings" and "don't know."

immigrant arrivals are viewed as having provided more benefits to the country than the later or "current" immigrant arrivals. Thus, Haitians and Cubans are currently perceived as particularly bad. So are the Iranians, but probably also because of the fear of terrorism that is associated with their country. Opinions about Koreans and Vietnamese have changed from a mainly negative to a generally positive view in the past decade.

Between 2001 and 2007, Americans were asked:

How satisfied are you with the treatment of immigrants in the United States?

As the data shown in Table 5.5 indicate there has been a decline in the percentage of Americans who are satisfied with the way immigrants are treated.

In 2006 and 2007 less than 50 percent expressed satisfaction with how immigrants are treated.

Among Hispanics the percent who indicated they were satisfied ranged from 44 to 25 percent.

On two especially controversial issues, whether illegal immigrants pay their fair share of taxes and whether they take jobs American workers want, a large majority of Americans, as shown below, believe they cost taxpayers too much, but less than 20 percent believe they take jobs Americans want.

On the first item, 65 percent of Hispanics in both years believe immigrants pay their fair share of taxes.

Two additional items focusing on illegal immigrants appeared on national surveys in 2007. The first asked:

In your view what should be the higher priority in dealing with the issue of illegal immigration: developing a plan for halting the flow of illegal immigrants in the U.S. or developing a plan to deal with illegal immigrants who are already in the U.S. or should both be given the same priority?

Table 5.5
How Satisfied Are You with the Treatment of Immigrants in the United States?

Year	Satisfied (%)	Dissatisfied (%)
2001	54	41
2002	55	39
2003	58	38
2005	54	42
2006	47	47
2007	43	50

Table 5.6
"Do Illegal Immigrants Pay Their Fair Share of Taxes?"

Year	Pay fair share of taxes	Cost taxpayers too much	Neither/Both No Opinion
2006	29	66	4
2008	31	63	6

Table 5.7
"Do Illegal Immigrants Take Jobs American Workers Want?"

Year	Take jobs American workers want	Take low-paying jobs American workers don't want	Neither/Both No Opinion
2006	17	74	10
2008	15	79	7

The majority, at 53 percent, answered that both should be given the same priority. Twenty percent favored a plan for halting the flow of illegals and 25 percent favored a plan to deal with illegals already in the country.

The second item asked:

In terms of dealing with illegal immigrants in the United States which of the following would you prefer to see happen: enforce the current laws more strictly and not pass new laws or pass new laws in addition to enforcing the current laws more strictly?

Here, the public was almost equally divided, 46 percent favored the first alternative (enforce current laws) and 50 percent favored the passage of new laws in addition to enforcing the current laws more strictly.

Finally, when asked in 2007:

How important is the issue of illegal immigration?

Thirty-five percent answered extremely important, 27 percent answered very important, 26 percent answered somewhat important, 7 percent not too important and 4 percent not at all important.

In summary, the data show that while most Americans do not want to have an increase in the number of immigrants admitted, a majority ranging from 52 to 67 percent believe immigration is a good thing for our country. And over the years, immigrants who arrived earlier are viewed more positively than any current group of immigrants. When asked between 2001 and 2007 how satisfied they were with the ways immigrants are treated, the results showed a decline from over 50 percent satisfied in the earlier years to 43 percent satisfied in 2007.

Concerning illegal immigrants, most Americans believe illegals cost the taxpayers too much but they do not take jobs that American workers want. More than half of the respondents, 53 percent, said the government's priority in dealing with illegals should be both dealing with a plan to halt additional illegals from entering the country and developing a plan to deal with those already here.

Respondents were almost evenly divided, 46 and 50 percent, on whether the government should enforce current laws *vis-à-vis* illegals more strictly and not pass new laws or pass new laws in addition to enforcing the current ones more strictly.

6

Public Opinion toward Abortion

The Federal law *vis-à-vis* abortions that applies today stems from the Supreme Court decision in *Roe v. Wade* 410 U.S. 113 (1973). According to the *Roe* decision adopted on January 22, 1973, with a 7 to 2 majority, most laws against abortion violated a constitutional right to privacy under the Due Process Clause of the 14th Amendment. The decision overturned all state and federal laws outlawing or restricting abortion that were inconsistent with its holdings.

The central holding of *Roe v. Wade* is that abortions are permissible for any reason a woman chooses, up until the "point at which the fetus becomes viable, that is potentially able to live outside the mother's womb, albeit with artificial aid." Viability is usually placed at about 28 weeks but may occur earlier even at 24 weeks. The Court also held that abortion after viability must be available when needed to protect a woman's health.

There were few laws on abortion in the United States at the time of independence, except the common law adopted from England, which held abortion to be legally acceptable if occurring before quickening.

Various anti-abortion statutes began to appear in the 1820s. In 1821, Connecticut passed a statute targeting apothecaries who sold poisons to women for purposes of abortion, and New York made post-quickening abortions a felony and pre-quickening abortions a misdemeanor eight years later. It is sometimes argued that the early American abortion statutes were motivated not by ethical concerns about abortion but by worry about the safety of the procedure. But some legal theorists believe that this theory is inconsistent with the fact that abortion was punishable regardless of whether any harm befell the pregnant woman and that many of the early statutes punished not only the doctors or abortionists, but also the women who hired them.[1]

Cases subsequently heard by the Supreme Court since *Roe v. Wade* include *Webster v. Reproductive Health Services, Planned Parenthood v. Casey, Stenberg v. Carhart,* and *Gonzales v. Carhart.*

In *Webster v. Reproductive Health Services* [492 U.S. 490 (1989)] in a 5-4 decision the Court declined to explicitly overrule *Roe v. Wade* because "none of the challenged provisions of the Missouri Act properly before us conflict with the Constitution."

In *Planned Parenthood v. Casey* [505 U.S. 833 (1992)] the central holding of *Roe v. Wade* was reaffirmed. The majority decision stated "At the heart of liberty is the right to define one's own concept of existence, of meaning, of the universe and of the mystery of human life."

During the 1990s, the state of Nebraska attempted to ban certain second-trimester abortion procedures sometimes called partial birth abortions. The Nebraska ban allowed other second-trimester abortion procedures called dilation and evacuation abortions. Justice Ginsburg stated, "this law does not save any fetus from destruction, for it targets only 'a method of performing abortion'." The Supreme Court struck down the Nebraska ban by a 5-4 vote in *Stenberg v. Carhart* [530 U.S. 914 (2000)], citing a right to use the safest method of abortion.[2]

In 2003, Congress passed the Partial-Birth Abortion Ban Act, which led to a lawsuit in the case of *Gonzales v. Carhart* [550 U.S. ___(2007)]. The Court had previously ruled in *Stenberg v. Carhart* that a state's ban on partial birth abortion was unconstitutional because such a ban would not allow for the health of the mother. The membership of the Court changed after *Stenberg,* with John Roberts and Samuel Alito replacing Rehnquist and O'Connor, respectively. Further, the ban at issue in *Gonzales v. Carhart* was a federal statute, rather than a relatively vague state statute as in the *Stenberg* case.

On April 18, 2007, the Supreme Court handed down a 5 to 4 decision *(Gonzales v. Carhart)* upholding the constitutionality of the Partial-Birth Abortion Ban Act stating that Congress was within its power to generally ban the procedure, although the Court left the door open for as-applied challenges.

Having reviewed the major Supreme Court decisions since *Roe v. Wade,* we turn now to an analysis of the public opinion data concerning abortion.

National Poll Data

The most recent poll conducted in July 2008 reported that 63 percent of the respondents support the *Roe v. Wade* decision and 33 percent oppose it. On abortion more generally, 19 percent believe abortion should be legal in all cases, 38 percent believe it should be legal in most cases, 24 percent responded that it should be illegal in most cases and 14 percent responded it should be illegal in all cases.

In 2006, in response to a CBS News poll that asked: "Under what circumstances do you believe abortion should be allowed?" 31 percent said they believed abortions should be permitted in all cases.

The earliest national poll data after *Roe v. Wade* revealed that in 1975, the same percentage of Americans (20 percent) believed abortion should be legal under any circumstances and that abortion should be illegal in all circumstances.

The next 15 years, from 1975 through 1990, Gallup recorded a gradual shift toward the more liberal position, with the percentage supporting abortion in all cases increasing to 31 percent and the percentage thinking it should be illegal in all cases dropping to 12 percent. Between 1991 and 1995, the balance of opinion at the extremes remained fixed at a two-to-one ratio, with roughly 33 percent taking the extreme pro-choice view and about half that number taking the extreme pro-life view.

In July 1996, coincident with the emergence of a new national debate over partial-birth abortion, Gallup recorded a significant drop in the number of Americans saying abortion should be legal in all cases. Since then, the percentage favoring unrestricted abortions has averaged just 25 percent, down from about 33 percent in the previous five years.

When asked in May 1987, May 1993, and February 2004: "Do you favor or oppose making it more difficult for a woman to get an abortion?" the results were as indicated in Table 6.1.

On each survey between 51 and 60 percent said they opposed making it more difficult for women to get an abortion.

When the answer to the question is broken by religion, we see in the percentage shown below that White Evangelical Protestants at 56 percent are most likely to favor making it more difficult and Jews at 12 percent and agnostics at 19 percent are least likely to favor making it more difficult.

In 1998, shortly before the 25th anniversary *of Roe v. Wade* 60 percent of respondents on a national poll said they thought the ruling was a good thing.

On the 30th anniversary of *Roe v. Wade*, a *CBS News/New York Times* 2003 poll found that 30 percent of respondents said abortion should be generally available, and 38 percent said it should be available but with stricter limits than now and 22 percent said it should not be available.

Table 6.1
"Do You Favor or Oppose Making It More
Difficult for a Woman to Get an Abortion?"

	May 1987 %	May 1993 %	Feb. 2004 %
Favor	**41**	**32**	**36**
Strongly	18	15	17
Not strongly	23	17	19
Oppose	**51**	**60**	**58**
Strongly	33	35	30
Not strongly	18	25	28
Don't Know	**8**	**8**	**8**

Table 6.2
"Do You Favor or Oppose Making It More
Difficult for a Woman to Get an Abortion?"

More Restrictions on Abortion

	Favor %	Oppose %	Don't Know %
White Evangelical Protestants	**56**	**39**	**5=100**
Attend weekly	63	31	6=100
Less often/Never	43	52	5=100
White Mainline Protestants	**27**	**64**	**9=100**
Attend weekly	33	58	9=100
Less often/Never	25	66	9=100
Black Protestants	**32**	**62**	**6=100**
Attend weekly	35	57	8=100
Less often/Never	29	67	4=100
Non-Hispanic Catholics	**36**	**56**	**8=100**
Attend weekly	50	44	6=100
Less often/Never	26	65	9=100
Hispanic Catholics	**35**	**59**	**6=100**
Attend weekly	43	51	6=100
Less often/Never	30	63	7=100
Jews	**12**	**87**	**1=100**
No Religion/Agnostic	**19**	**76**	**5=100**

Table 6.3
"Should Abortion Be Generally Available, Available but with
Stricter Limits Than Now, Not Available?"

	Generally Available %	Available But with Stricter Limits %	Not Permitted %
March 1993	42	36	24
May 2000	37	39	22
March 2001	33	43	23
March 2003	39	38	22

When the same question was asked in March 1993, May 2000, and March 2001, the results looked like this.

In each year, less than 25 percent of the respondents believed abortions should not be permitted.

Over the years, since the *Roe v. Wade* decision there have been little if any differences in the opinions of men and women *vis-à-vis* abortion. Differences accrued among respondents of different religious groups, most notably Evangelical Christians who have been consistently and strongly opposed to abortion.

We conclude by noting that *Roe v. Wade*, some thirty-five years since its adoption, still enjoys public support.

Notes

1. *http://en.wikipedia.org/wiki/Abortion_in_the_United_States*: (Suzanne M. Alford, "Is Self-Abortion a Fundamental Right?" (*http://www.law.duke.edu/shell/cite.pl?52+Duke+L.+J.+1011*), 52 Duke Law Journal 1011, accessed October 16, 2008.
2. "South Dakota Readies Again for Abortion Fight." *Washington Post*, September 4, 2008, p. A3.

7

Public Opinion toward Affirmative Action

Affirmative action is composed of a range of policies used to combat differences among groups in earnings and employment opportunities.[1] It emerged from a concern for equal employment opportunities (EEO). The first conscious attempt by the government to address this issue took place in the late 1940s, when it became illegal to withhold federal employment on the basis of race and ethnicity.[2] The basic statutory framework for affirmative action in employment and education derives from the 1964 Civil Rights Act, which subjects private and public employers to equal employment opportunity regulations.[3] Eventually, these policies aiming at equal access for minorities and women to employment included their active recruitment to job and education opportunities. In the 1960s, state and local governments attempted to follow suit with the federal government through designing their own affirmative action programs and policies.[4] However, the history of affirmative action in the U.S. can be traced back to hundreds of years ago, depending on how one defines the term. For example, the Bureau of Refugees, Freedom, and Abandoned Lands, established in 1865, was a temporary agency set up to help newly freed black citizens in their transition from slavery to freedom. In addition, other groups have historically received preferential treatment in public services such as health and education. These groups include veterans, athletes, and descendents of graduates, well before the modern era.[5]

Affirmative action, perceived as giving special preference to particular groups as a means to achieving equality, has been a point of contention in American politics for decades. This issue remains a focal point as the constitutional status of affirmative action has reached the Supreme Court in a number of critical cases. In 1978, in *Regents of University of California v. Bakke*, the Supreme Court held that the use of restrictive racial quotas was impermissible under the Equal Protection Clause of the Fourteenth Amendment.[6] Until the present, public debate still surrounds the federal and Supreme Courts consideration of Affirmative Action policies. The issue at hand was the constitutionality of these programs, especially when it comes to admissions policies to colleges and universities. The Supreme Court concluded in 2003, in *Grutter v. Bollinger*, that the benefits that result from a diverse student body justify the consideration of race in a university's admissions decision. However, in *Gratz v. Bollinger*, the Court decided that "racial bonus points" to minority applicants are unconstitutional.

National Poll Data

Amidst these debates and disagreements, public opinion toward affirmative action gains special importance. It is difficult to summarize the state of public opinion toward this issue. The public's opinion toward affirmative action appears to be highly affected by the way the question is worded, particularly when the question describes the programs in more detail.[7] On the one hand, there is support for the rationale of affirmative action—such as overcoming past discrimination or increasing the diversity of the student body in colleges and universities. This is reflected in the general support for the idea of affirmative action. But at the same time Americans question the fairness of such programs. In addition, Americans are generally sensitive when the question mentions special preferences to minority groups. This is probably a function of the American culture, which believes in equality of opportunity. The following figures from a 2002 Pew Survey show how Americans are supportive of affirmative action, but are divided regarding the fairness of such programs.

These figures show that a majority of Americans favor affirmative action to help minorities and women get better jobs (63 percent). The percentage drops slightly when special preferences in hiring and education are mentioned (57 percent). A majority (60 percent) perceives affirmative action as good, while only 30 percent perceives it as bad. However, only 47 percent perceives it as fair, while 42 percent perceives it as unfair. And only 24 percent favor giving blacks and other minorities preferential treatment.

Similar results were reflected in a 2003 Pew survey, in which 60 percent said that affirmative action programs are good and only 30 percent said they were bad. But respondents were divided as to whether these programs were fair (47 percent) or unfair (42 percent). When the sample is broken by gender, similar results occur, with a slight majority of women saying that affirmative action is fair (52 percent). When break-

Table 7.1
Varied Responses to Affirmative Action

In order to overcome past discrimination, do you favor or oppose affirmative action programs...		
...designed to help blacks, women, and other minorities get better jobs and education?	Favor Oppose DK/Ref	63 29 <u>8</u> 100
...which **give special preferences** to qualified blacks, women, and other minorities in hiring and education?	Favor Oppose DK/Ref	57 35 <u>8</u> 100
All in all, do you think affirmative action programs **designed to increase the number of black and minority students on college campuses:**		
...are a good thing or a bad thing	Good Bad DK/Ref	60 30 <u>10</u> 100
...are fair, or unfair	Fair Unfair DK/Ref	47 42 <u>11</u> 100
We should make every possible effort to improve the position of blacks and other minorities, even if it means **giving them preferential treatment.***	Agree Disagree DK/Ref	24 72 <u>4</u> 100
*Asked in July 2002		

ing the sample by race, we find that the majority of whites (54 percent), blacks (87 percent), and Hispanics (77 percent) still perceive affirmative action as a good thing. However, the majority of non-whites, blacks, and Hispanics believe these programs are fair. The majority for Hispanics is sizeable. This should draw attention to the centrality of race in framing discussions around affirmative action.

There is also an increasing trend in the support for affirmative action.

The figures above from Gallup's annual Minority Rights and Relations poll show an increase in support for affirmative action from 1995

Table 7.2
Affirmative Action Programs

	Good %	Bad %	DK %	Fair %	Unfair %	DK %	(N) %
Total	60	30	10 =100	47	42	11=100	(1201)
Sex							
Male	54	36	10	43	48	9	(577)
Female	65	24	11	52	35	13	(624)
Race							
White	54	35	11	45	43	12	(1021)
Black	87	5	8	58	35	7	(80)
Hispanic	77	17	6	70	27	3	(77)

Table 7.3
Affirmative Action Support Grows

Affirmative Action Support Grows

Preferences not mentioned	August 1995 %	2003 %
Favor	58	63
Oppose	36	29
DK/Ref	3	8
	100	100
"Special Preferences"		
Favor	46	57
Oppose	46	35
DK/Ref	8	8
	100	100

to 2003, although the increase is slight. The figure below shows these developments (Jones, 2005).

This increasing trend could be attributed, at least in part, to the continued perception of a significant effect of race on the probabilities of advancement for racial minorities. A 2008 USA Today/Gallup poll found most Americans say racism is widespread against blacks in the U.S. This

Opinion of Affirmative Action Programs for Racial Minorities

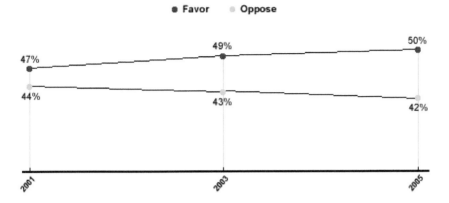

Do you think racism against blacks is or is not widespread in the U.S.?

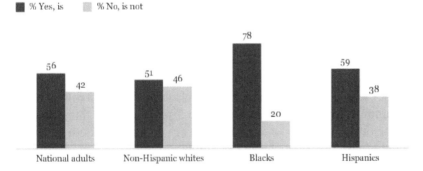

USA Today/Gallup poll, June 5–July 6, 2008

GALLUP POLL

includes a slight majority among whites (51 percent), a slightly higher majority among Hispanics (59 percent), and a large majority among blacks (78 percent).

The data in Table 7.4 indicate that between 2003 and 2007 a large majority of blacks believe white students have better chances of gaining admission to major U.S. universities, although whites were more likely to say that both groups have equal opportunities.

For the three surveys shown above, there was little fluctuation in the perceptions of whites and blacks. More than 60 percent of the blacks thought that a white student who is equally qualified as a black student is

Table 7.4
If Two Equally Qualified Students, One White and One Black, Applied to a Major U.S. College or University, Who Do You Think Would Have the Better Chance of Being Accepted to the College—[ROTATED: the White Student, the Black Student]—or Would They Have the Same Chance?

	White student	Black student	Same chance	No opinion
Total	%	%	%	%
2007 Jun 4-24	29	22	43	6
2005 Jun 6-25	29	20	47	4
2003 Jun 12-18	31	29	36	4
Non-Hispanic Whites				
2007 Jun 4-24	20	26	48	6
2005 Jun 6-25	21	24	50	5
2003 Jun 12-15	24	34	38	4
Blacks				
2007 Jun 4-24	61	5	28	6
2005 Jun 6-25	64	4	29	3
2003 Jun 12-18	67	5	24	4

more likely to gain admission to a major U.S. university. The percentage of black respondents who thought that a black student had a better chance of gaining admission was no more than 5 percent in the three surveys. On the other hand, whites were more likely to think that both groups of students have the same chances of admission.

It should also be noted that this slight increase in support for affirmative action masks important differences by gender, race, and political affiliation. Women are more supportive of affirmative action (66 percent) than men (48 percent). And men are more likely to oppose these programs (41 percent) compared to women (26 percent). Also women are more likely to perceive programs that increase the number of minority college students as a good thing (60 percent) as compared to men (48 percent). Forty-three percent of the men perceive these programs as a bad thing, while only 28 percent of women perceive them as such.

The differences become clearer when approaching the issue of support for affirmative action from a race-based perspective. The figure below shows the support of Americans for affirmative action since Gallup started to ask this question in 1995. Blacks had a stable trend of not favoring a reduction in affirmative action (the percentages range from 6 percent to 11 percent). On the other hand, the percentages of whites who support

Table 7.5
Gender Gap on Affirmative Action

Programs that… help blacks, women, and other minorities get jobs and education	White Women %	White Men %
Favor	66	48
Oppose	26	41
Don't Know	8	11
	100	100
…raise # of minority college students		
Good thing	60	48
Bad thing	28	43
Don't Know	12	9
	100	100

Source: 2003 Pew Survey.

Percentage Who Would Like a "Decrease" In Affirmative
Action Programs, by Race

In general, do you think we need to increase, keep the same, or decrease
affirmative action programs in this country?

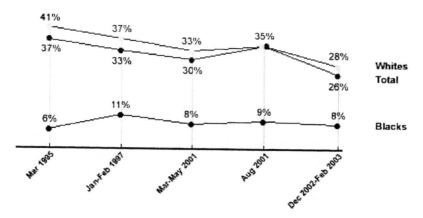

a decrease in affirmative action programs have a wider range (26-41). Interestingly, since 1995, the gap between whites and blacks on affirmative action is the smallest in 2003.

This narrowing gap could be attributed to liberalizing trends sweeping American society as well as generational differences. These trends are reflected in Pew's 2004 survey on political trends in the U.S. society. For example, since 1987 Americans are increasingly accepting of interracial dating according to Pew's surveys as shown in the figure below. The generational gap is also clear from majority support for interracial dating among younger generations.

According to a 2003 Pew survey, 85 percent of the baby boomer generation supported interracial dating in 2002/2003. Agreement among the younger generation (born starting 1977 and later) was even higher (91 percent). As will be clarified shortly, liberals are more likely to support affirmative action. Therefore, these liberalization trends among younger generations could be used to explain the increasing trend in support for affirmative action.

The idea that younger generations are more supportive of affirmative action is further supported by the decreasing percentage of agreement with the phrase "We have gone too far in pushing for equal rights in this country" when moving from older to younger generations. The figures below come from the same Pew survey.

There is also a clear division in support for affirmative action by party affiliation. Conservative republicans are more likely to perceive affirmative action as bad (54 percent), while a large majority of liberal

I think it's all right for blacks and whites to date each other

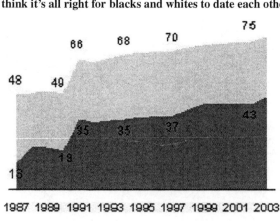

"I think it's all right for blacks and whites to date each other"			
	percent agreeing		
Generation	1987-88	2002-03	Change
Born pre-1913	26%	—	—
WWII (1913-1927)	31%	49%	+18
"Silent" (1928-1945)	41%	60%	+19
Boomer (1946-1964)	59%	77%	+18
Gen X (1965-1976)	64%	85%	+21
Gen Y (1977-)	—	91%	—
Total	**48%**	**76%**	**+27**

"We have gone too far in pushing equal rights in this country"			
	percent agreeing		
Generation	1987-88	2002-03	Change
Born pre-1913	49%	—	—
WWII (1913-1927)	52%	50%	-2
"Silent" (1928-1945)	47%	58%	+11
Boomer (1946-1964)	38%	48%	+10
Gen X (1965-1976)	34%	42%	+8
Gen Y (1977-)	—	34%	—
Total	**43%**	**46%**	**+3**

democrats are likely to perceive it as good (77 percent). Also a majority of liberal democrats perceive affirmative action as fair, while 62 percent of the conservative republicans perceive it as unfair.

Republicans are also more likely to think that the U.S. has gone too far in pushing equal rights, as shown in the trend in the figure below from a Pew survey. The gap started widening since the early 1990s.

Opinion on the Impact of Affirmative Action

Despite this trend toward support for affirmative action, it is important to note the perceptions of those affected by affirmative action. In the 2003 Pew survey mentioned above, only 15 percent reported having

Table 7.6
Support for Affirmative Action by Party Affiliation

Party Ideology	Good	Bad	DK		Fair	Unfair	DK	(N)
Conservative Rep.	36	54	10		26	62	12	(2223)
Moderate Republican	57	31	12		47	41	12	(132)
Cons./Mod. Democrat	61	26	13		55	33	12	(184)
Liberal Democrat	77	22	1		66	32	2	(86)

We have gone too far in pushing equal rights in this country
(white respondents only)

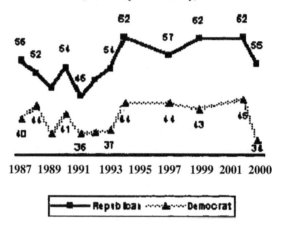

been directly affected by affirmative action. Overall, 11 percent report having been hurt, and 4 percent report that they were helped. Among the blacks, 14 percent say they have been helped, and 5 percent report having been hurt. Only 2 percent of the whites report having been helped by affirmative action programs, while 13 percent report that they were hurt. Four percent of the Hispanics say they were helped, while 4 percent said they were hurt.

These results draw attention to the interaction effect between the social stigma attributed to affirmative action and the need of minorities, especially black, for the assistance gained through affirmative action.

Overall, the issue of Affirmative Action continues to divide American public opinion, especially along gender, racial, and ideological lines. Women, minorities, and liberals are more likely to support affirmative action. This trend is supported by continued perception of racial dis-

Table 7.7
Personally Affected by Affirmative Action?

	Helped %	Hurt %	Not Affected %	Other/Don't Know %
All	4	11	82	3=100
Whites	**2**	**13**	**84**	**1=100**
Men	1	17	81	1=100
Women	3	9	86	2=100
Liberals	7	15	76	2=100
Moderates	2	10	87	1=100
Conservatives	1	14	83	2=100
Black	**14**	**5**	**77**	**4=100**
Hispanic	**4**	**8**	**87**	**1=100**

crimination in the U.S. as well as liberalizing trends among the younger generations. The effects of racial and ideological dividing lines have been stable since the 1990s. But while the gap between whites and blacks regarding the idea of affirmative action has recently slightly narrowed, the effects of ideological dividing lines remained more or less stable.

It should also be noted that Americans are generally supportive of affirmative action. But support drops when details of specific programs are mentioned, or when preferential treatment is included in the question. This in part shows that framing affirmative action programs and discourse as an attempt to increase equality could gain more support than framing the issue as an attempt to account for historical discrimination.

Notes

1. Coate, Stephen and Clenn C. Loury. 1993. Will Affirmative-Action Policies Eliminate Negative Stereotypes? *The American Economic Review.* 83(5). pp. 1220-1240.
2. Kellough, J. Edward. 1992. Affirmative Action in Government Employment. *Annals of the American Academy of Political and Social Science.* 523. September. 117-130.
3. Dale, Charles V. 2005. Affirmative Action Revisited. In Peterson, James S. *Affirmative Action: Federal Laws, Regulations and Legal History.* New York: Novinka Books.
4. *Op Cit.* Kellough.
5. Beckman, James M. 2006, *Affirmative Action: An Encyclopedia.* New York: Greenwood Press.

6.   *Op. Cit..*
7.   Jones, Jeffrey M. 2005. Race, Ideology, and Support for Affirmative Action. Available through:
       http://www.gallup.com/poll/18091/Race-Ideology-Support-Affirmative-Action.aspx. Access Date: September 23, 2008.

8

The United States between 1945 and 1954: A New World Order with Mounting Challenges and Anxieties

The decade following World War II witnessed major events that arguably shaped history during the following four decades. These years ushered in the end of an era and the beginning of a new one. The era that ended was that of European dominance over world affairs, followed by an era in which the locus of global power shifted to the United States and its rival power, the Soviet Union. The "iron curtain" fell between the East and the West, and the Cold War officially started when the Soviet Union tested its first nuclear weapon in 1949.

President Franklin D. Roosevelt had died in April 1945, and was succeeded by Harry S. Truman, who was his running mate in the presidential elections of 1944. Much to the surprise of the pollsters who predicted a victory for Thomas Dewey, Governor of New York, over Truman in the 1948 election, Truman was elected. Truman's presidency witnessed the first use of nuclear weapons against Japan in 1945, which contributed to putting a decisive end to the Second World War. On August 6 and 9, 1945, President Truman authorized dropping two atomic bombs on Hiroshima and Nagasaki, after 6 months of intense fire-bombing of sixty-seven other Japanese cities. These bombs killed almost a quarter of a million people, in addition to injuries and sicknesses that led to more deaths and birth defects for years to come. Japan announced its surrender less than a week later. Germany had surrendered in May, 1945, after Hitler's suicidal death in April of the same year.

The Nuremberg trials, conducted between 1945 and 1949, represented a watershed for establishing an international regime for holding individuals and governments responsible for war crimes. A panel of judges from the United States, the United Kingdom, France, and the Soviet Union held German leaders personally responsible for war crimes including aggression and crimes against humanity, in addition to a series of other charges.

On another front, the UN Conference on International Organization began in San Francisco on April 25, 1945. The delegates of fifty nations convened at this conference to ratify the United Nations Convention. The Charter of the International Court of Justice was also ratified at the same conference. With the establishment of the United Nations, a new world order was created.

But the building blocks of the Cold War era were also accumulating rapidly. President Harry Truman instructed the State Department to open the negotiations leading to the creation of the North Atlantic Treaty Organization, NATO, in 1949. As had become common practice during the Cold War years, the Soviet Union responded by creating its own alliance, the Warsaw Pact, in 1955. At an earlier date, Secretary of State George Marshall devised the European Recovery Plan, known as the Marshall Plan, to aid rebuilding of war-torn Europe as a way of protecting the continent from Soviet influence. Truman approved the plan in 1948, and from that date until 1952, Europe received about $13 billion from the United States. Containing the spread of Communism was the guiding principle of these programs.

In May, 1948, following a U.N. resolution in 1947, the state of Israel was established and formally recognized a few hours later by the United States. The Soviet Union recognized Israel shortly afterwards.

The Korean War started in 1950, and rapidly developed into a confrontation between the two superpowers—the United States and the Soviet Union, joined later by China in 1950. The fighting concluded three years later with no change in borders. But the huge number of casualties and the Communist challenge that materialized during the war left their impact for years to come. Before the Korean War officially ended in 1953, the United States had already exploded the first hydrogen bomb on November 1, 1952.

Another shocking event that took place during this period was the assassination attempt on President Truman by two Puerto Rican nationalists on November 1, 1950. Their goal was to draw attention to the cause of Puerto Rican independence. The attempt failed, leading to the death of a White House police officer and one of the assassins. The second assassin received life imprisonment.

These events had their impacts on U.S. politics and society. The 1952 Supreme Court opinion in *Youngstown Sheet and Tube Co. v. Sawyer* aimed at strengthening the jurisdictional limitations on the president's authority, including during war time. The case was initiated by steel companies against the president's Executive Order directing the Secretary of Commerce to seize and operate most of the steel mills in anticipation of a nation-wide strike of steel workers in April 1952. The Order was based on the powers of the president as the chief executive and commander-in-chief of the Armed Forces, arguing that the strike could negatively affect the war effort in Korea. The Court ruled that "[t]here is no statute that expressly authorizes the President to take possession of property as he did here. Nor is there any act of Congress to which our attention has been directed from which such a power can fairly be implied."[1]

This ruling, which attempted to protect private property rights against intrusion by the Executive, came against the backdrop of the 1947 Labor-Management Relations Act—widely known as the Taft-Hartley Act—which basically curbed the rights of labor versus business owners. This Act was passed over President Truman's veto, and led to curbing many rights provided by the 1935 National Labor Relations Act, known as the Wagner Act. The latter Act only prohibited "unfair labor practices" committed by employers. On the other hand, the Taft-Hartley Act prohibited a wide range of union political and advocacy activities, including union donations to federal political campaigns.

Cold War anxieties also dominated other fields of public life. Allegations of being a Soviet agent or sympathizer became powerful weapons used against political adversaries. The term McCarthyism refers to this state of distrust and Communist fears that spread widely in political and cultural circles during the 1950s. The term was coined after the Republican senator from Wisconsin Joseph McCarthy who, as Chairman of the Senate's Government Committee on Operations, conducted a large number of investigations in various government departments and questioned the political allegiances of office holders. These investigations led many public officials and civil servants to lose their positions, and became a symbol for ideological terrorism and manipulating national security issues to serve political ends. To a large extent, these anti-Communist politics were directed against the Democratic Party, and helped Eisenhower win the presidential election of 1952 against Adlai Stevenson, who was accused of being too soft on Communists. However, support for McCarthy's accusations soon began to fade given the absence of concrete evidence. In 1954, the Senate voted to censure the Republican senator.

On the civil rights front, one of the most significant events during this decade was the 1954 U.S. Supreme Court ruling in *Brown v. Board of Education*. The Court's opinion aimed at ending racial segregation in public schools by ruling that "separate but equal" is inherently unequal. Needless to say, this goal was not easily achieved, and was met by intense opposition. Many judges throughout the south gave the narrowest possible interpretation to the racial integration mandate, and the majority of southern black students continued to attend overwhelmingly black schools. The ruling, however, was the cornerstone for the ensuing political and legal confrontations between support and opposition groups of civil rights and equality for blacks. These confrontations had started earlier, but were given shape and new directions as a result of this Supreme Court ruling. Violence erupted, the Civil Rights movement developed, and civil disturbances led the federal government to deploy army troops in Memphis to control the uprising of obstructionists. Clearly the years between 1945 and 1954 created the ground for much unrest and confrontations in the decades that followed.

Public Opinion Data 1945-1954

African Americans

One of the earliest questions asked on national polls about African Americans was whether "Negroes are as intelligent as Whites?" to which 52 percent answered that they are.

Additional questions during the decade 1945-54 included: "Do you disapprove of separate sections on buses?," to which 49 and 50 percent answered that they disapproved in 1945 and 1949; "Do you support federal intervention to required nondiscriminatory hiring?," to which one third responded that they did "all the way" in 1948, 1949, and 1950; and finally, when asked "Do you think most Negroes in the United States are being treated fairly or unfairly" two thirds answered "fairly" in 1946.

Jews

One of the earliest questions included on national surveys about attitudes toward Jews concerned how much power they have in the United States. In 1946, 55 percent of the respondents said they thought Jews "have too much power in this country."

When asked between March 1945 and November 1954: "Have you heard any criticism or talk against the Jews in the last six months?" The percent answering "yes" ranged from 14 to 62. In March 1945 and February 1946, 62 and 64 percent answered "yes," but between November 1950 and November 1954 the percent dropped to 14.

On specific issues such as "How would you feel about marrying a Jew?," in 1950, 57 percent said they would definitely not marry a Jew.

And when asked: "Suppose a Jewish family were going to move in next door to you. Would you say you wouldn't like it at all, or that you wouldn't like it but it wouldn't matter too much or that it wouldn't make any difference to you?"

Between 3 and 10 percent said they "would not like it at all" and between 69 and 88 percent said "it wouldn't make any difference."

Immigration

What has become the basic question asked of the American public on immigration is: "Should U.S. Immigration Policy be kept at its Present Level, Increased, or Decreased?"

In 1946 and 1953 the results were as follows:

Years	More/Increase	Same/ Present Level	Fewer/ Decrease	None	No Opinion/ Don't Know
1946*	5	32	37	14	12
1953	13	37	39	--	11

*In 1946 the question was phrased: "Should we permit more persons from Europe to come to this country each year than we did before the war, should we keep the number the same, or should be reduce the number. "None" was a choice only in 1946.

Over the seven-year time period, the percentage of respondents who favored increasing immigration increased from 5 percent to 13 percent, and those who favored maintaining it at its "present" level increased by 5 percent. In 1946 a majority of the respondents, 51 percent, favored decreasing the number of immigrants or not allowing any immigrants to enter the United States compared to 39 percent who advocated decreasing the number in 1953.

Sources

Canon, Bradley C., and Charles A. Johnson. 1999. *Judicial Policies: Implementation and Impact.* Second Edition. Washington, DC: CQ Press.

Note

1.   U.S. Supreme Court. *Youngstown Sheet and Tube Co. v. Sawyer.* Available through: *http://caselaw.lp.findlaw.com/scripts/getcase.pl?navby=case&court-us&vol=343+&page=579.* Access Date: October 15, 2008.

9

The United States between 1955 and 1964: Institutionalizing Civil Rights and Cold War Interactions

The 1950s witnessed an era of economic prosperity and population growth. It also witnessed confrontations and violence on the Civil Rights front.

On December 1, 1955, a bus driver ordered Rosa Parks and three other blacks to give up their seats to free room for a white passenger. Having refused to obey the order, the driver contacted the police and signed a warrant for their arrest. This arrest gave rise to the Montgomery Bus Boycott, which lasted until December 20, 1956.

The Civil Rights Movement found this incident a suitable opportunity to take the issue to the judiciary. Four black citizens brought a class action lawsuit against the city commissioners, chief of police, state public service commission, a common carrier, and its drivers, challenging the constitutionality of laws that require the segregation of the white and colored races on city motor buses. The case, known as *Browder v. Gayle,* was heard before the U.S. District Court for the Middle District of Alabama. Based in part on *Brown v. Board of Education*, the Court ruled that the "separate but equal" doctrine was no longer a correct statement of the law. Accordingly, the court ruled that statutes and ordinances requiring segregation on motor buses violated the Fourteenth Amendment's due process and equal protection clauses. This case put an end to the boycott of bus transit in Montgomery, but led to more violence as segregationists attacked buses, black churches, and homes of civil rights activists.

The Little Rock crisis represented another important event in the Civil Rights Movement during this decade. Following on the Supreme Court's ruling in *Brown v. Board of Education*, the National Association for the

Advancement of Colored People (NAACP) registered nine black students, later known as the Little Rock Nine, to attend the previously all-white Little Rock Central High School. But segregationists threatened mass protests, and the State Governor deployed the Arkansas National Guard on September 9, 1957, to block the nine black students from reaching their school. The incident attracted national attention, and raised the polarizations between the two groups supporting and opposing racial integration. President Eisenhower intervened and summoned the Arkansas governor to meet him.

Attorneys from the U.S. Justice Department requested an injunction against the governor, which was granted, and the District Court for the Eastern District of Arkansas ordered the governor to withdraw the National Guard on September 20. The police then slipped the students into their schools, and confronted the protesting parents of white students. On September 24, President Eisenhower ordered the deployment of army troops in Little Rock, and federalized the Arkansas National Guard to ensure the safety of the Little Rock Nine and enforce integration.

Another event that helped spread the Civil Rights cause was the so-called Greensboro sit-ins in 1960. Sit-ins were an established technique for the Civil Rights Movement given its overall nonviolent approach to social change. However, these sit-ins were the most influential because of the media attention they attracted and their broad scope. The events leading to the protest started in February 1960, when four students from North Carolina Agricultural and Technical State University (NC A&T), a historically segregated school, were denied the right to sit down in the Woolworth lunch counter. They were told that because of their race they had to stand up at another counter to eat. The young men stood and stayed until the store closed, and students returned to sit-in the next day. This protest continued for six months, joined by other similar protests in different cities and states. While many local stores changed their policies regarding racial segregation, the main legal change had to await the passage of the landmark Civil Rights Act of 1964, which was followed by the Voting Rights Act of 1965.[1]

In 1960, the Supreme Court joined the legal battle for civil rights through its ruling in *Boynton v. Virginia*. In this case the Court found that the assignment of facilities in interstate and rail stations based on race constituted discrimination, and thus was unconstitutional.[2] Following on this ruling, the Congress of Racial Equality (CORE) undertook a symbolic tactic to mark the legal end of segregation. In 1961, seven blacks and six whites left Washington, DC on two public buses headed to the

South. On their journey the travelers encountered violence and met with hostility from angry crowds. Despite the violence, CORE leaders thought that stopping the ride would send a wrong message. They reinforced the remaining riders with volunteers, and the trip continued. They were savagely attacked by a mob of more than 1,000 whites in Montgomery. The extreme violence and the indifference of local police prompted a national outcry of support for the riders, who faced still more violence, even jail, as they continued their journey.

This long ride inspired people all over the country. The Interstate Commerce Commission responded by issuing rules that prohibited segregation in transportation facilities.[3] Hope for change mounted with the election of John F. Kennedy as president in January 1961 after defeating Vice President and Republican candidate Richard Nixon. These elections witnessed the first televised presidential debates in U.S. history.

The Montgomery bus boycott, and other events especially since *Brown v. Board of Education*, encouraged more resistance in industrialized and highly-segregated Birmingham, Alabama. This city was often in the center of the struggle for civil rights not only because of its citizens' efforts to institute these rights, but also because of staunch opposition from its local government. The Alabama Christian Movement for Human Rights, led by Reverend Fred L. Shuttlesworth, invited Martin Luther King Jr. to participate in a campaign to protest segregation by businesses and the city's refusal to institute racial integration policies. The city's Mayor used fire hoses and dogs against nonviolent black activists. After being arrested during the demonstrations, King wrote his famous "Letter from a Birmingham Jail," responding to the critics of the movement. Finally, following several weeks of demonstrations, civil rights and business leaders agreed on a settlement that reduced segregation in the city. Segregationists conducted more violence, which led to loss of lives. But civil rights issues were already high on the agenda.

Other symbolic events followed. The first two African American students, James Hood and Vivian Malone Jones, enrolled in the University of Alabama in June 1963, against opposition from some state officials, including the governor. The two students were escorted into the university by federalized National Guard troops. The following day civil rights leader Medgar Evers was shot to death in Jackson, Mississippi. Two years later, Jones became the first black to graduate from the University of Alabama in its 134 years of existence.[4]

The activism and violence that developed in Birmingham and elsewhere inspired the nation and speeded up steps for important legal developments.[5] In order to show support for President Kennedy's proposed civil rights bill, which was part of his election campaign promises, civil rights groups organized a march on Washington, DC. Over 250,000 people from around the nation arrived in the capital in more than 30 special trains and 2,000 chartered buses on August 28, 1963. Martin Luther King, Jr., delivered the closing address, his famous "I Have a Dream" speech. No violence took place during that day, and the event was an overwhelming success that drew extensive media coverage.[6]

Efforts toward institutionalizing civil rights reached a high point by the end of this decade through the issuance of the Civil Rights Act in 1964. The provisions of this Act forbade discrimination on the basis of race or sex in hiring, promoting, and firing. Title VII of the act created the Equal Employment Opportunity Commission (EEOC) to implement the law.[7] The Act also prohibits discrimination on the basis of race, color, and national origin in programs and activities receiving federal financial assistance. In addition, it also provided for the integration of schools and other public facilities. The Act was signed into law by President Lyndon Johnson on July 2, 1964. At around the same time, the Freedom Summer campaign was organized in the summer of 1964 to register blacks in the Deep South to vote. As had happened before in other campaigns, especially in the South, white segregationists initiated violence that led to the loss of lives.[8]

This political vigor transferred to student movements as well when, in 1962, the Students for a Democratic Society was created—a counter-cultural movement that was collectively known as the new left.[9] The Berkeley Free Speech Movement was another manifestation of this vigor. This was led in part by the increasing numbers of leftist students on a number of campuses. Generally, the aims of these students were to end nuclear testing, capital punishment, Cold War rivalries, and other perceived social ills. Student activism in Berkeley led to restrictive university policies as well as security interference. A change in the University's administration allowed students more freedom of expression and political organization.[10]

The most tragic event in this decade, and probably one of the most tragic events in American history, took place on November 22, 1963. This was the assassination of President Kennedy. Although investigations led to the conviction of Lee Harvey Oswald, the case remains controversial until today. Following Kennedy's assassination, Vice President Lyndon Johnson became president.

Johnson showed his determination to follow in President Kennedy's footsteps by encouraging Congress to eliminate racial discrimination, end poverty and hunger in the United States, provide federally-financed health insurance through Medicare and Medicaid, and increase funding for education. As part of the so-called Great Society policies, Johnson implemented the War on Poverty program in 1964, hoping to eliminate poverty in the United States. The results of these programs were mixed, as will become clear in later years, especially given their tax burdens.[11] Combined with the deteriorating situation in the Vietnam war, as will be explained in the next section, Johnson's popularity dwindled, leading to his decision not to seek reelection in the 1968 presidential race.

On the Cold War front, the so-called Hungarian uprising started on October 23, 1956 against the pro-Soviet government in the country, and was quickly crushed by Soviet military intervention on November 10 of the same year. The U.S. deference, except for verbal criticism, to this invasion signaled the acceptance of separate zones of influence for the two superpowers in Europe. And while it alienated many Marxists in Europe and elsewhere, it strengthened the Soviet control over its sphere of influence on the continent.

The significance of the Hungarian uprising becomes clear when compared to the Suez crisis, which also took place in 1956. Responding to the decision by Egypt's President Nasser to nationalize the Suez Canal, Britain, France, and Israel coordinated an invasion of the country that started on October 29, 1956. The situation was different in this case compared to that in Hungary. In the latter case, the United States had to acquiesce to the exercise of Soviet influence within its sphere of influence. In the Suez case, both the United States and the Soviet Union sent strong messages to Britain and France that the era of their dominance was over. The Soviet Union and other Warsaw Pact nations threatened to intervene on the Egyptian side. In response, President Eisenhower threatened to use "everything in the bucket" if the invading parties continued their operations. On November 6, Britain and France agreed to the cease fire.

This invasion was also a landmark in the process of decolonization, which was another reflection of the end of European dominance over international politics.

Given the power vacuum that resulted from the demise of the British and French influence in the Middle East following the Suez crisis, and the increasing Soviet influence in the Arab world, especially in Egypt and Syria, President Eisenhower announced the Eisenhower Doctrine on January 5, 1957 in a speech to the Congress. The doctrine stipulated that a country can request American economic assistance and/or military aid if it is threatened by armed aggression from another state. The doctrine singled out Soviet threat in particular by authorizing the commitment of U.S. forces "to secure and protect the territorial integrity and political independence of such nations, requesting such aid against overt armed aggression from any nation controlled by international communism."[12] The Doctrine also required wielding war-making power to the president.

The first application of the Eisenhower Doctrine also came in the Middle East, in response to the 1958 Lebanon crisis. The country was threatened by a civil war between Christian Maronites and Muslims. These tensions resulted from the pro-Western policies of Lebanese President Camille Chamoun, who requested U.S. assistance to prevent attacks from his rivals, who were basically Muslims, Communists, and/or nationalists, and allegedly supported by the newly created United Arab Republic comprised of Egypt and Syria. President Eisenhower responded by sending army troops to Lebanon, which successfully quelled the opposition. Although the Eisenhower Doctrine was never referred to during the crisis, this operation signaled to the Soviet Union that the United States would act to protect its interests in the Middle East.[13]

Another critical event that took place during this decade and marked a turning point in the Cold War era was Castro's takeover of power in Cuba in December 1958. The Cuban Revolution overthrew Dictator Fulgencio Batista, and established a pro-Soviet Communist regime on America's doorstep. The U.S. policy toward the new communist regime consisted largely of isolating the country through economic sanctions.[14]

Amidst these competitive rivalries, Soviet Premier Nikita Khrushchev visited the United States and met President Eisenhower in September 1959. As later events showed, this visit reflected the ability of both countries to compromise on critical issues and establish an international regime that allowed for understanding, direct negotiations, and mutual restraint. The Eisenhower-Khrushchev visits carried hopes that a new communications system between the East and the West may be developing.[15] The first U.S. exhibition in the Soviet Union was created in 1959 as a result of negotiations between Vice President Nixon and Premier Khrushchev.[16] In 1961, the Peace Corps was created to promote world peace and friendship between the United States and other developing countries.[17]

Shortly after his inauguration, President Kennedy permitted a band of Cuban exiles, armed and trained in the United States, to invade their homeland. This attempt, widely known as the Bay of Pigs invasion, was a failure.[18] The Charter of Punta del Este was adopted in August 1961, creating the Alliance for Progress. The Alliance was initiated by President

Kennedy as an international economic development program established by the United States and twenty-two Latin American countries.[19] One main goal of this program was to counter communist influences in Latin America, especially with the new regime in Cuba. A couple of years later, in August 1963, the Berlin wall was erected. It became a symbol of the Cold War divide and a material manifestation of the Cold War's Iron Curtain between the East and the West.[20] Soon after, the new president had to face the most severe crisis in the Cold War era that threatened the whole world with nuclear annihilation.

In October 1962, U.S. Air Reconnaissance discovered that the Soviets had installed nuclear missiles in Cuba. Kennedy demanded from the Soviet Union the removal of all missile bases and ordered a blockade of the island country in order to stop further Soviet shipping of missiles and other materials. In response, Soviet Premier Nikita Khrushchev authorized Soviet field commanders in Cuba to launch tactical nuclear weapons if invaded by American forces.[21] Later, Kennedy agreed with Khrushchev to withdraw the missiles and save the world from a nuclear confrontation. The threat presented by this crisis convinced the leaders in both countries that the spread of nuclear weapons can lead to destructive results. This contention led to the test ban treaty of 1963.[22]

Events were also developing on the Vietnam front during this decade, leading to the protracted conflict that pitted the Communist government of North Vietnam and its allies in South Vietnam, known as the Viet Cong, against the government of South Vietnam and its principal ally, the United States. This war was clearly a part of Cold War rivalries, in which the United States and the Soviet Union were deeply involved. At the heart of the conflict was the desire of North Vietnam, which had defeated the French colonial administration of Vietnam in 1954, to unify the entire country under a single communist regime.

With the de facto partition of Vietnam in 1954 according to the Geneva accords, President Eisenhower decided to provide large assistance to South Vietnam. Kennedy's Administration saw Vietnam as a critical arena in which the United States should prove its ability to counter Communist expansion. The administration based its logic on the domino theory, which stipulated that Southeast Asian countries were closely linked and that a communist success in one country must necessarily lead to the fatal weakening of other countries.

Convinced that Premier Diem's regime in South Vietnam was ineffi-cient, corrupt, and unable to face the Northern threats, the United States signaled its tacit acceptance to an army coup that overthrew Diem. The situation continued to deteriorate further, and the U.S. military presence came under attack from the North. President Johnson ordered retaliatory air strikes against Northern Vietnamese naval bases, and requested Congress to authorize the president to take whatever action he deemed necessary to deal with future threats to U.S. forces or allies in Southeast Asia. The measure, dubbed the Gulf of Tonkin Resolution, passed the Senate and House overwhelmingly on August 7. In November, Johnson was elected president through a landslide victory.[23]

Cold war rivalries were also present on the scientific front. On October 4, 1957, the Soviet Union launched Sputnik I, the world's first artificial satellite, thus ushering in a new era of U.S.-Soviet confrontation known as the space race. Later the same year, on November 3, the Soviet Union caught world attention once more, as well as American fears, by launching Sputnik II, this time carrying the dog Laika, the first mammal to orbit the Earth. The tide turned in favor of the U.S. with the successful launch of Explorer I. This mission succeeded in discovering the magnetic radiation belts around the Earth. The U.S. reaction to Sputnik led to the creation of the National Aeronautics and Space Administration (NASA) in October 1958.[24] On another scientific front, Dr. Jonas Salk developed a vaccine for Polio—a highly contagious disease that spreads through human contact and can attack the nervous system and lead to paralysis.

Public Opinion 1955-1964

African Americans

When asked in the next decade about Negro intelligence, the percentage who answered they are as intelligent as whites increased from 52 percent to 77 percent.

Concerning school segregation in 1956, 1963, and 1964, 49, 62, and 63 percent of respondents answered that they believed white and Negro students should go to the same schools.

And concerning their approval or disapproval of the *Brown v. Board of Education* decision between 55 and 62 percent expressed their approval of the Court's decision.

Comparing responses of southerners and non-southerners to the question: "Are you opposed to having your child attend a school in which a majority of the pupils are Negroes?" between 53 and 57 percent of non-southerners were opposed in contrast to between 81 and 83 percent of southerners.

As for segregation on public transportation, between 59 and 79 percent expressed disapproval. The 79 percent occurred in 1963.

Between 51 and 61 percent of the respondents said it would make no difference to them "If a Negro moved into their block" between 1955 and 1964.

On the extent of "Pro-integration Sentiments Expressed in 1963," the percentages are shown below:

Guttman Scale of Prointegration Sentiment, 1963

Item	Prointegration Percentage
1. Do you think Negroes should have as good a chance as white people to get any kind of job, or do you think white people should have the first chance at any kind of job?	82
2. Generally speaking, do you think there should be separate sections for Negroes in streetcars and buses?	77
3. Do you think Negroes should have the right to use the same parks, restaurants, and hotels as white people?	71
4. Do you think white students and Negro students should go to the same schools or to separate schools?	63
5. How strongly would you object if a member of your family wanted to bring a Negro friend home to dinner?	49
6. White people have a right to keep Negroes out of their neighborhoods if they want to, and Negroes should respect that right.	44
7. Do you think there should be laws against marriages between Negroes and whites?	36
8. Negroes shouldn't push themselves where they're not wanted.	27

Adapted from Paul B. Sheatsley, "White Attitudes Toward the Negro," *Daedalus* (Winter 1966), 217-237, at p. 224. Reprinted by permission of *Daedalus*, Journal of the American Academy of Arts and Sciences, Boston, MA, Winter, 1966. *The Negro American-2*. To quote Sheatsley: "The properties of a Guttman scale are such that if a person rejects one item on the scale, the chances are at least nine in ten that he will reject the items below it. Thus, whose who reject the top item-equal job opportunities for Negroes—are highly unlikely to endorse any of the other items on the scale and may be considered extreme segregationists. At the other end of the scale, the 27 percent who disagree with the proposition that 'Negroes shouldn't push themselves where they're not wanted' are extremely likely to take a prointegration position on all seven of the other items."

Concerning reactions to the 1960s Civil Rights demonstrations, between 58 and 80 percent thought they "hurt" Negro rights.

The table below shows the percentage of respondents who disapproved of various tactics used in the demonstrations.

Activity/Item	Disapproval Percentage Nationwide
Summer 1963	
Lie down in front of truck at construction sites to protest hiring discrimination	91
Sit-in at lunch counters	67
Go to jail to protest discrimination	56
Boycott products whose manufacturers don't hire enough Negroes	55
Summer 1964	
1. This summer white and Negro students are going to Mississippi to organize Negroes to vote. Do you generally approve of this move or disapprove of it?	57
2. Do people approve or disapprove of picketing of political conventions as occurred at the Cow Palace in San Francisco?	76
3. People have different views about the Negro demonstrations. Some people say the Negroes should stop their demonstrations now that they have made their point and even though some of their demands have not been met. Others say they have to continue demonstrating in order to achieve better jobs, better housing, and better schools. With which view do you agree?	
(Stop demonstrating.)	73

Finally, when asked again in 1956 whether "Negroes are being treated fairly," two thirds answered, "Yes, they are treated the same as whites."

Jews

On the issue of Jewish power in the United States, in 1962 and 1964, 17 and 13 percent thought "Jews have too much power in this country."

When asked if they "heard any criticism or talk against the Jews in the last six months, between 11 and 14 percent in 1955 through 1959 answered "yes."

In 1962, when asked a series of questions about the admirable and objectionable qualities that characterized Jews, 78 percent of the respondents did not mention any objectionable qualities. As for the admirable qualities, the two most frequently mentioned were ability in business and finances (13 percent) and racial and religious loyalty (16 percent).

In 1964, items that have become known as the Anti-Semitic Index were asked for the first time. The specific items and the percent who answered in a manner indicating anti-Semitic attitudes are shown below.

The percent providing anti-Semitic responses ranged from 13 to 63 percent. Item 9, "Jews always like to be at the head of things," at 63 percent, Item 10, "Jews stick together too much," at 58 percent and "International banking is pretty much controlled by Jews," at 55 percent had the greatest anti-Semitic responses. Only 13 percent thought "Jews have too much power in the U.S."

Statement	1964
1. Do you think Jews have too much power in the U.S.	13
2. Do you think Jews have too much power in the business world.	33
3. Jews are more willing than others to use shady tactics to get what they want.	48
4. Jews are more loyal to Israel than to America.	39
5. Jews are not as honest as other businessmen.	30
6. Jews have a lot of irritating traits.	48
7. International banking is pretty much controlled by Jews.	55
8. Jews don't care what happens to anyone but their own kind.	30
9. Jews always like to be at the head of things.	63
10. Jews stick together too much.	58
11. The trouble with Jewish businessmen is that they are so shrewd and tricky other people don't have a chance in competition.	40

Asked in 1992, 1998, and 2002 instead of #7 "Jews have too much control/influence on Wall St."

In 1962, 4 percent of respondents answered "yes" when asked "Should colleges limit the number of Jews they admit?"

When asked "How would you feel about marrying a Jew?," 37 percent answered that they would "definitely not marry a Jew."

And on the issue of how they would feel about having a Jewish family move in next door to them, 95 percent said that it "wouldn't make any difference."

Notes

1. Greensboro Historical Museum. Available through: *http://www.greensborohistory.org/exhibits/exhibits_sitins.html*. Access Date: October 22, 2008.

2. The U.S. Supreme Court. Available through: *https://blackboard.american.edu/webapps/portal/frameset.jsp?tab_id=_2_1&url =%2Fwebapps%2Fblackboard%2Fexecute%2Flauncher%3Ftype%3DCourse% 26id%3D_47594_1%26url%3D*. Access Date: October 22, 2008.

3. Congress for Racial Equality. Available through: *http://www.core-online.org/History/freedom%20rides.htm*. Access Date: October 22, 2008.

4. Douglas Martin. 2005. Vivian Malone Jones, 63, Dies; First Black Graduate of the University of Alabama. *The New York Times*. October 14.

5. Black History. Available through: *http://www.africanaonline.com/civil_rights_birmingham.htm*. Access Date: October 23, 2008.

6. African American History. Available through: *http://www.watson.org/~lisa/blackhistory/civilrights-55-65/marchwas.html*. Access Date: October 23, 2008.

7. The National Archives. Available through: *http://www.archives.gov/education/lessons/civil-rights-act/*. Access Date: October 22, 2008.

8. Congress of Racial Equality. Available through: *http://www.core-online.org/History/freedom_summer.htm*. Access Date: October 23, 2008.

9. For more on the political debates and differences during the 1960s, see: Michael W. Flamm and David Steigerwald. 2008. *Debating the 1960s: Liberal, Conservative, and Radical Perspectives*. Lanham: Rowaman & Littlefield Publishers, Inc.

10. David Burner. 1996. *Making Peace with the Sixties*. New Jersey: Princeton University Press.

11. Ohio History Central. Available through: *http://ohiohistorycentral.org/entry.php?rec=1822*. Access Date: October 23, 2008.

12. The U.S. Department of State. Available through: *http://www.state.gov/r/pa/ho/time/lw/82548.htm*. Access Date: October 20, 2008.

13. The U.S. Department of State. Available through: *http://www.state.gov/r/pa/ho/time/lw/82548.htm*. Access Date: October 20, 2008.

14. CRS Report for Congress. 2007. Cuba: Issues for the 110th Congress. Available through: *http://fpc.state.gov/documents/organization/94107.pdf*. Access Date: October 21, 2008.

15. *Time*. Available through: *http://www.time.com/time/magazine/article/0,9171,825955,00.html?iid=chix-sphere*. Access Date: October 21, 2008.

16. U.S. Department of State. Available through: *http://www.state.gov/p/eur/ci/rs/c26473.htm*. Access Date: October 21, 2008.

17. The Peace Corps. Available through: *http://www.peacecorps.gov/index.cfm?shell=learn.whatispc.mission*. Access Date: October 23, 2008.

18. The White House. Available through:
http://www.whitehouse.gov/history/presidents/jk35.html. Access Date: October 21, 2008.

19. *Britannica*. Available through:
http://www.britannica.com/EBchecked/topic/16355/Alliance-for-Progress#tab =active~checked%2Citems~checked&title=Alliance%20for%20Progress%20-- %20Britannica%20Online%20Encyclopedia. Access Date: October 23, 2008.

20. *Berlin Wall Online*. Available through:
http://www.dailysoft.com/berlinwall/. Access Date: October 22, 2008.

21. *History and Politics Out Loud*. Available through:
http://www.hpol.org/jfk/cuban/. Access Date: October 21, 2008.

22. The White House. Available through:
http://www.whitehouse.gov/history/presidents/jk35.html. Access Date: October 21, 2008.

23. For more information, see *Britannica*. Available through:
http://www.britannica.com/EBchecked/topic/628478/Vietnam-War/234630/The- Diem-regime-and-the-Viet-Cong#tab=active~checked%2Citems~checked&tit le=Vietnam%20War%20%3A%3A%20The%20Diem%20regime%20and%20t he%20Viet%20Cong%20--%20Britannica%20Online%20Encyclopedia. Access Date: October 23, 2008.

24. NASA. Available through:
http://history.nasa.gov/sputnik/. Access Date: October 20, 2008.

10

The United States between 1965 and 1974: A Decade of Opportunities and Strife

The decade between the years 1965 and 1974 presented windows of opportunity for some groups, and tragedies and lingering conflicts for others. In the policy arena, windows opened for more government intervention, which was manifested at the beginning of this decade by launching the Medicare program. As windows opened in one policy area, they transferred momentum to others. The earlier successes of the civil rights movement inspired the gay and lesbian community, who revolted in New York against police harassment and continued interference with places where homosexuality was known to be accepted. On the other hand, the civil rights movement, which so far refers mainly to the rights of blacks, witnessed the shocking and tragic assassination of one of America's most revered figures—Martin Luther King, Jr. While dreadful and alarming, this assassination was not the only violent incident that disturbed the nation during this decade and caught it off guard. Violence during this decade was mainly incited by ethnic tensions, the continued involvement in Vietnam, and the new intervention in Cambodia. The assassinations of Malcolm X, Martin Luther King, Jr., and Robert Kennedy remained, as the case with President Kennedy's assassination, controversial.

An important window opened for a larger government role as a result of the circumstances that accompanied the reelection of incumbent President Johnson. The so-called Goldwater debacle gave the Democrats majorities in both Houses of Congress, and allowed them to pass many of their proposed Great Society policies and programs. The "debacle" was named after Senator Barry Morris Goldwater, or "Mr. Conservative," as he was sometimes called by the media. Senator Goldwater attempted to unite the Republican Party against Big Government, and what was seen as the New Deal-style policies of President Johnson. The landslide victory of incumbent President Lyndon Johnson shocked the Republican Party, especially given the loss of many of its seats in Congress to a young and energetic group of Democratic politicians. The American Conservative Union was established in December 1964 as an attempt to resurrect the Conservative movement.[1] But the Republican Party had to wait for almost a decade and a half after this defeat to rise to prominence under the leadership of Ronald Reagan.

In the meanwhile, the new liberal seats in Congress allowed the Johnson Administration to enact many of its promised programs under the umbrella of the Great Society. These included Medicare, Medicaid, the poverty program, and aid to education.[2] These programs entailed major spending, but many of them survived until today, most notably Medicare and Medicaid, in addition to the government's expanded role in education.

This century also witnessed the launch of a new movement—the gay rights movement. Until the 1950s and 1960s, homosexuals were regularly arrested by the police, which could mean becoming blacklisted from government employment. The new window was supported by the rise of the new left, as discussed in the previous section, and the edge gained by the Democratic Party in recent elections.[3] It is also arguable that the general atmosphere during this decade, which was rampant with violence, demonstrations, and assassinations, was conducive to the arrival of this movement.

While attempts at mobilization started earlier in the decade, the real launch of the gay rights movement had to await the Stonewall riot to show momentum and ability to organize. In the summer of 1969, the New York police raided the Stonewall Inn, a popular gay bar in the Village. While police raids at gay bars were common, this time riots followed. Crowds gathered outside the bar, and riots spread rapidly. The following year, a march was organized in New York City in commemoration of these riots.[4] The Gay Liberation Front (GLF) was created in New York City in 1969.[5] Other gay, lesbian, and bisexual civil rights organizations were also formed as a reaction to the Stonewall riots.[6]

The feminist movement had made earlier gains compared to the gay rights movement. A window of opportunity was opened during the previous decade through President Kennedy's ideas and policies, which aimed at elevating the status of women and establishing gender equality. As mentioned in the previous section, the Civil Rights Act banned discrimination based on gender. The Equal Pay Act, which was passed in 1963, also made it illegal to pay women less than men.[7] On

October 29, 1966, the National Organization for Women was created in Washington, DC to sponsor the call for gender equality and "to bring women into full participation in the mainstream of American society."[8] This organization inspired the creation of other women's organizations throughout the country.

A slightly related, but highly relevant, incident during this decade was the approval by the Food and Drug Administration of birth control pills in 1960. Birth control generally will become an important issue of contention in U.S. politics and society.[9] As had become a common practice, the Supreme Court intervened early on, this time to protect the right of families to the use of contraception as a matter of privacy. In 1965, in *Griswold v. Connecticut*, the Supreme Court provided opinion on a Connecticut statute which makes it a crime for any person to use any drug or article to prevent conception. The Court ruled the law unconstitutional based on the right to privacy.[10] In 1972, the Supreme Court ruled in *Eisenstadt v. Baird* that the right to privacy includes an unmarried person's right to use contraceptives.[11] Besides these rulings, it is arguable that the most critical case related to women's rights during this decade, which also had long-term repercussions, was the Court's ruling in *Roe v. Wade*, which established women's rights to safe and legal abortions. This ruling overrode anti-abortion laws in many states, and led to massive mobilizations across the country as well as instances of violence.[12]

The Civil Rights front remained on top of the scene, but with staggering tragedies this time. The decade witnessed numerous race riots in Nebraska, Illinois, Mississippi, Florida, Massachusetts, Georgia, New Jersey, Alabama, and California.[13] The Watts Riots of 1965 reflected the continued state of antagonism and ethnic tension that characterized the national mood. The riots started when a California Highway patrol officer stopped a young African American man for suspicious driving and suspicion of being drunk. Crowds started to gather and police reinforcements arrived to handle the increasingly involved assemblage. The incident quickly turned violent as Officer Wayne Wilson dispatched with force both brothers in the car, Marquette and Ronald Frye. The news quickly spread, and as the mother, Rena Frye, arrived, the first blows were being delivered. The three family members were taken away for resisting arrest. The ensuing violence led to the death of thirty-four people, in addition to damaging or looting hundreds of buildings.[14]

Another significant incident of racial riots took place in Newark, New Jersey between July 12 and 17, 1967. The social and political exclusion of blacks, in addition to brutality and violence, exploded in riots and major civil disturbance that claimed 43 lives, 33 of them black, and hundreds of buildings were destroyed.[15] The catalytic event of these riots was not very different from the one that incited Watts about two years earlier. John Smith, a black cab driver was arrested for tailgating a police car, and was allegedly beaten by police who accused him of resisting arrest. A crowd gathered outside the police station where he was detained, and the rumor spread that he had been killed while in custody. Civil disturbances erupted soon afterwards.[16]

Such incidents were alarming in the sense that they led to highlighting the ongoing social divide and lingering tensions. In 1966, Kwame Ture, the civil rights leader known as Stokely Carmichael, coined the phrase "black power" as part of a Pan African ideology. He had been chosen as Chairman of the Student Nonviolent Coordinating Committee (SNCC), which was created following the Greensboro sit-ins of the previous decade. Unlike his predecessor, John Lewis, Ture rejected the tactics of passive resistance and called for black separatism. His arguments found resonance with disillusioned blacks, who were also sympathetic to the urgings of Malcolm X, who had been assassinated a year and a half earlier, that the struggle should be carried out by any means necessary. These ideas ignited a white backlash and alarmed an older generation of civil rights leaders, including Martin Luther King, Jr.[17]

The assassination of Malcolm X in 1965, which is sometimes attributed to tensions among black leaders, was the first tragedy in the Civil Rights Movement during this decade. The assassination of Martin Luther King, Jr. on April 4, 1968, is probably one of the most tragic incidents in the nation's history. As with other assassinations, conspiracy theories were quickly woven around the incident. Riots and violence soon erupted in more than 100 cities. April 7 remains a national day of mourning. Fifteen years after the assassination of King, President Ronald Reagan signed a bill into law making the third Monday of January, King's birthday, a national holiday celebrating his birth and life. The campaign for this honor began soon after his assassination.[18]

Robert Kennedy, President John Kennedy's younger brother and trusted advisor, was also assassinated in the same year. He was shot dead on June 5, 1968, after winning California's Democratic presidential primary.[19] He had announced his candidacy for the Presidency on March 16, 1968.[20] A few days before his death, on April 4, Robert Kennedy mourned the death of Martin Luther King, Jr. after hearing the news of his assassination while delivering a speech in a black neighborhood in Indianapolis.[21]

These elections witnessed another shock. The withdrawal of President Johnson from the presidential race caught Americans by surprise, although it was not highly unexpected given the deterioration of the war situation in Vietnam and the war crimes committed by the American army there. This, in addition to the later invasion of Cambodia under Nixon, set another wave of demonstrations, riots, and civil disturbances.

Before discussing these disturbances, it makes sense to review the war situation in Vietnam, which kept draining American power for years to come. The Soviet Union was watching at a distance, supporting the anti-American forces, and clearly satisfied with seeing the American troops sinking deeper in the mud of Vietnam, something that the United States would be more than willing to pay back to the Soviets during their involvement in Afghanistan the following decade. But the ally that the United States supported against the Soviet invasion in Afghanistan proved highly resistant to annihilation and difficult to understand. This ally-turned-enemy developed into global terrorism under the cloak of Islam, and proved highly evasive and costly to fight. More importantly, as will be explained later, it threatened to change the American way of life by American hands when counter-terrorism became an excuse for violating human rights and Constitutional values.

American combat troops were deployed in Vietnam in 1965 to prevent the South Vietnamese government from collapsing.[22] Now the United States had delved deeper into the war to the extent of actual engagement. The anti-war demonstrations, which gained national prominence by 1965, soon turned into a social movement that remained powerful until the end of the war. This movement united a number of groups that were sometimes sufficiently different to the extent that they displayed animosity. These groups included college students, leftist organizations, people from the middle class, labor unions, and government institutions.[23] On a number of occasions, the anti-war demonstrations deteriorated into incidents of intense violence.

Two main events during the second half of the 1960s contributed immensely to the anti-war movement as well as the anti-war sentiments among the American public. The first was the Tet offensive, a massive attack on the Viet Cong and the North Vietnamese, which ended in the defeat of the Communists. But the scale of the attack and the losses endured by the American troops left the American public convinced that the war had been lost. The result seemed to be a loss of the will to fight, a detrimental situation for any war effort.[24]

The war effort represented the main pretext for passing the 26th amendment to the Constitution of the United States on March 23, 1971. Draftees into the armed services were all young males over the age of eighteen. But the Fourteenth Amendment set the voting age at twenty-one. Now that young men starting at the age of eighteen are required to fight and die for their country, it did not seem correct to deprive them of their voting rights. First, Congress attempted to right this wrong in 1970 by passing an extension to the 1965 Voting Rights Act, giving the vote to all persons eighteen or older, in all elections, on all levels. Oregon objected to this change. In December 1970, a divided Supreme Court decided in *Oregon v Mitchell* that the Congress had the power to lower the voting age to 18 for national elections, but not for state and local elections. A few months later, the Congress passed the amendment.[25]

The second detrimental incident that contributed to the public pressures to end the war was the news about the My Lai Massacre, in which the American army was involved in killing hundreds of unarmed civilians in the Vietnamese village of My Lai on the morning of March 16, 1968. Earlier leakages had convicted the American army of committing war crimes and using internationally illegitimate weapons in Vietnam. But the proven atrocities in My Lai, which were confirmed by eyewitness reports, sent a shockwave throughout the American political and military establishment, and further divided a public already wary of the human, economic, and moral costs of the war. The story of this massacre was made public in November 1969.[26] It was the cover story in both *Time* and *Newsweek*, and graphic photographs were released. Army investigators later discovered three mass graves containing the bodies of about 500 villagers. In the end, however, only few would be tried and only one, William Calley, would be found guilty. President Nixon ordered Calley removed from the stockade (after spending a single week there) and placed him under house arrest. On November 9, 1974, the Secretary of the Army announced that William Calley would be paroled. These decisions further enraged the public.[27]

On another Cold War front, two wars shook the Middle East and opened windows for confrontations between the two superpowers. The first was the Israeli attack and occupation of lands in four Arab countries. On June 5, 1967, the Israeli army launched coordinated attacks that ended with the occupation of the Egyptian Sinai Peninsula, the Syrian Golan Heights, the Jordanian-controlled West Bank, Egyptian-controlled Gaza strip, and the remaining parts of historical Palestine, including East Jerusalem, which remained outside of Israeli control after the war of 1948.

UN Security Council Resolution 242 called on Israel to withdraw from Arab lands occupied in 1967. This war intensified the Cold War boundaries in the Middle East. President Nasser of Egypt severed diplomatic ties with the United States for its support of Israel during the war, and invited Soviet military experts to Egypt. While the situation changed on the Egyptian front after less than seven years, the situation on other fronts is still provoking violence in the region and elsewhere in the world.

The second war started on October 6, 1973, when the Egyptian and Syrian armies, backed by unprecedented support from other Arab countries, launched a surprise coordinated attack against the Israeli occupation of Sinai and the Golan Heights. The so-called Yom Kippur war led to moving the situation on the stalemated Arab-Israeli front. While the war on the Syrian front continued until 1974 without any border changes, the UN Security Council Resolution 338 in 1973 calling for a cease fire was recognized on the Egyptian front. This Resolution was issued after negotiations between the two superpowers who sought to calm the situation in the region and avoid confrontation.

While foreign wars in other regions were never a direct concern to the American public, the Yom Kippur war attracted public attention and concern. Unlike the case with the Vietnam War, the reason was not American casualties or moral concerns, but was rather related to the Arab oil embargo initiated by a number of oil producing countries in support of the Egyptian and Syrian war efforts. This embargo, which included raising the price of oil by OPEC for countries supporting Israel, exposed the vulnerability of the United States and drew attention to the issue of energy conservation. Dependence on Middle Eastern oil has become an important issue of contention in American presidential elections ever since.

Johnson's failure to calm the situation on the Arab-Israeli front was not his main failure. The failures in Vietnam, which escalated other economic burdens at home, contributed to loss of rigor that he had gained at the beginning of the decade. The domestic pressures rose from internal strife, civil disorder, and anti-war sentiments. Coupled with the embarrassing war crimes committed in Vietnam, Johnson realized that he did not have a chance in the presidential election of 1968. Before announcing his withdrawal from the presidential race, Johnson ordered a pause of almost all bombing of North Vietnam. Negotiations with North Vietnam began in Paris the same year, leading to the Paris Peace Accords in 1973 during Nixon's Presidency.[28] These accords ended direct U.S. involvement and stopped the fighting between the North and South, at least for a while.

Richard Nixon won the Presidency in 1968 in one of the tensest moments of American history. The public was still angered over the assassination of two of its most important leaders who brought a promise of hope to the political arena—Martin Luther King, Jr. and Robert Kennedy. Racial violence, anti-war sentiments, and rejectionist ideologies contributed to this tense atmosphere. The violence that erupted in the Democratic Convention in Chicago in 1968 attests to these boiling feelings.[29] Despite a number of foreign policy successes, including ending the war in Vietnam and rapprochement with China, the Nixon era witnessed tensions arising from the Vietnam war, interference in Cambodia, and, most shattering of all, the Watergate scandal. Nixon is still the only president in American history to resign from office.

The American public was further disillusioned and alienated from its government by the expansion of the Vietnamese war into officially neutral Cambodia. The aim of the American incursion into Cambodia was to destroy Communist bases in the country. This neutrality, which was already precarious, was strongly shaken by the coup led by Cambodian premier, General Lon Nol, against the country's ruler, Prince Norodom Sihanouk. When the new government tried to expel the North Vietnamese and Viet Cong from their bases on the Cambodian-Vietnamese border, fighting broke out. The Northern Vietnamese Army and Viet Cong were assisted by the growing forces of the Communist-inspired Khmer Rouge movement. The Americans and South Vietnamese were eager to strike at this potential Communist stronghold, in addition to their desire to destroy a sanctuary and supply route for the Northerners.

The allied operations began on April 29, 1970. President Nixon had promised that this would be a limited attack for the sole purpose of preventing offenses against South Vietnam. By the end of June, the American forces ended their operations, leaving widespread controversies and bitter sentiments among the public. The most tragic event linked to this invasion was the so-called Kent State massacre, in which the Ohio National Guard shot at students at Kent State University who were protesting the war on Cambodia. Four students were killed and nine others were wounded. Now the war had come home, a process that had started earlier and culminated in Kent state with the fall of civilian victims.[30]

The Cold War witnessed a number of important transformations during Nixon's Presidency. Most notably was Nixon's visit to China in February 1972. At the conclusion of the president's trip, the American and Chinese governments issued the "Shanghai Communique," a statement of their foreign policy views. The two nations pledged to work toward the full normalization of diplomatic relations. The United States acknowledged the Chinese "One China Policy" and that Taiwan is part of China. The statement enabled the two countries to temporarily set aside the "crucial question obstructing the normalization of relations"—Taiwan—and to open trade and other contacts. In May 1973, the United States and China established the United States Liaison Office (USLO) in Beijing and a counterpart Chinese office in Washington, DC.[31]

This opening of relations was critical for the Cold War atmosphere. The strain in the Sino-Soviet relations had surfaced starting the second half of the 1950s. American diplomacy was successful in capitalizing on this situation in order to widen the distance between the two Communist powers and bring China into closer relations with the United States against the expansion of Soviet influence. Despite the rapid developments in these relations, they remained an issue of contention in the United States, first as a result of China's human rights record and, later, for issues related to the trade balance between the two countries.

On the other hand, steps toward détente between the United States and the Soviet Union began to progress starting in the second half of the 1960s. These steps were reflected in increased trade and cooperation with the Soviet Union and the signing of the Strategic Arms Limitation Treaty Agreement (SALT I).[32] The second round of talks leading to SALT II started in 1972. These steps were facilitated by the policies of Leonid Brezhnev.[33] Brezhnev however was dedicated to the struggle against the United States, which assured the Soviet bureaucracy and guaranteed its support. In 1968, he ordered the invasion of Czechoslovakia to crush the Prague Spring, justifying the move by what came to be called the "Brezhnev Doctrine," asserting Moscow's right to intervene in the affairs of other socialist states.[34] This explains why the Soviet Union was unable to use the opportunity of the détente to strengthen its economy, and its overextension in the Third War, culminating in the decision to invade Afghanistan, which had fatal consequences for the former super power.

As the decade opened by the shocking and much grieved assassinations of Malcolm X, Martin Luther King, Jr., and Robert Kennedy, in addition to tragic racial violence, civil disturbances, and huge losses in Vietnam, the closing years of this decade witnessed one of the most devastating political scandals in American history—the Watergate Scandal. In 1972, Nixon was running for a second term in office, which he won against Senator George McGovern.[35] But this time, the story did not finish there. The chain of events that took place over the following two years led to the first resignation of an American president in the history of the country.

The scandal started to unfold when five burglars broke into the Democratic Party's National Committee offices in the Watergate hotel on June 17, 1972. Because of the possibility that the Federal Interception of Communications statute had been violated, the DC police called in the FBI, which suspected that the burglars were in the process of installing listening devices in the Democratic Party offices. Investigators later determined that this was the second illegal entry into the Democratic Party's headquarters. A group of burglars had earlier installed wiretaps and photographed documents.[36] Two of the burglars were James McCord and G. Gordon Liddy, both members of the Committee to Re-Elect the President (CREEP). A third suspect was E. Howard Hunt, a former CIA agent and White House aide.[37] The White House attempted to obscure the investigations in what is known as the "cover up," which led to more abuses of power.

These early events did not affect Nixon's campaign, and he was heading for reelection in the fall of 1972. But by the summer of 1973, the Watergate affair was a full-blown national scandal and the subject of two official investigations, one led by Special Prosecutor Archibald Cox, the other by North Carolina Senator Sam Ervin, chairman of the Senate Watergate Committee. The most critical revelation during the investigations came in July 1973, when a White House aide testified that Nixon had a secret taping system that recorded his phone calls and conversations in the Oval Office. When Nixon refused to release the tapes, Ervin and Cox issued subpoenas. The White House refused to comply, citing "executive privilege," the doctrine that the president, as chief executive, is entitled to candid and confidential advice from aides.[38] But the pressures kept building.

Nixon's last days in office came in late July and early August, 1974. The House Judiciary Committee voted to accept three of four proposed Articles of Impeachment, with some Republicans voting with Democrats to recommend impeachment of the president. The final blow came with the decision by the Supreme Court to order Nixon to release more White House tapes. One of these tapes revealed that Nixon had participated in the Watergate cover-up as far back as June 23, 1972. Calls for Nixon's resignation spread across the country. At 9pm on the evening of August 8, 1974, Nixon delivered a nationally televised resignation speech.[39] Vice President Ford assumed the Presidency, and issued a pardon for Nixon, an action that angered public opinion but helped put an end to the ongoing controversies.

Despite the tragic incidents that this decade has witnessed, it did not end without "one small step for (a) man, one giant leap for mankind."

These were the words of Neil Armstrong on arriving on the moon, on July 21, 1969. Neil Armstrong and Edwin Aldrin were the first humans to set foot on the moon on Apollo 11, a step that converted science fiction into reality.[40]

Public Opinion: 1965-1974

African Americans

On the matter of separate schools, by 1965, two thirds of the respondents thought white and Negro students should go to the same schools.

When non-Southern respondents were compared against Southern respondents on the issue of whether they opposed sending their child to a school where a majority of the pupils were Negros there were no differences in responses in 1966 and 1969 but in 1965 and 1970, 76 v. 52 and 69 v. 51 percent of the Southerners opposed the practice.

In 1965 and 1966, 62 and 49 percent of the respondents said it would make no difference to them if a Negro moved into their block.

A majority of the respondents, and in 1966 and 1967, a large majority (86 and 89 percent), believed that the Civil Rights demonstrations hurt Negro rights.

When asked "How well do you think Negroes are treated in this country—the same as whites are, not very well, or badly?" 72 and 70 percent in 1967 and 1968 answered the same as whites.

Finally, in 1973, slightly more than half of the respondents (53 percent) believed that black/white relations will always be a problem in the United States.

When the public was asked between 1965 and 1970 whether they opposed sending their child to a school where a majority of the children were Negro, between 54 and 76 percent of respondents living in the South said they were opposed. In contrast, between 59 and 51 percent of persons living in other parts of the country said they were opposed.

In March 1970, 81 percent of respondents said they opposed "the busing of Negro and white children from one school district to another."

In 1965 and 1966, the public was asked if it would make any difference to them if a Negro moved into their block to which 62 percent in 1965 but only 49 percent in 1966 said it would make no difference.

In response to the Civil Rights demonstrations that were occurring in major cities throughout the country, 86 and 89 percent of respondents thought they were hurting Negro rights.

On the general issue of how well respondents thought Negroes were treated in this country in 1967 and 1968, 72 and 70 percent thought they were treated as well as whites. These responses are slightly higher than those reported in the mid 1940s and 1950s.

Looking into the future when asked "What is the likelihood that a solution to the problem of black/white relations in the United States will ever be worked out," 53 percent in 1973 said "it will always be a problem."

Jews

Items that were part of the anti-Semitic index were included on a national survey in 1969 with the following results.

Anti-Semitic Index (Percent)

Statement	1969
1. Do you think Jews have too much power in the U.S.	11
2. Do you think Jews have too much power in the business world.	26
3. Jews are more willing than others to use shady tactics to get what they want.	28
4. Jews are more loyal to Israel than to America.	29
5. Jews are not as honest as other businessmen.	30
6. Jews have a lot of irritating traits.	30
7. International banking is pretty much controlled by Jews.	35
8. Jews don't care what happens to anyone but their own kind.	40
9. Jews always like to be at the head of things.	42
10. Jews stick together too much.	52
11. The trouble with Jewish businessmen is that they are so shrewd and tricky other people don't have a chance in competition.	54

Asked in 1992, 1998, and 2002 instead of #7 "Jews have too much control/influence on Wall St."

"Jews stick together too much" (52 percent) and "The trouble with Jewish businessmen is that they are so shrewd and tricky other people don't have a chance in competition" (54 percent) were the most widely-held views. Only 11 percent thought that Jews had too much power in the U.S.

Immigration

No questions on immigration appeared on national polls between 1955 and 1964. In 1965, the public was asked again about whether they favored an increase, decrease, or no change in the number of immigrants permitted to enter the country. The results looked like this

	Percent
Increase	8
Present Levels	39
Decrease	33
No Opinion	20

Again, less than 10 percent favored increasing immigration.

On the basic question reported in the 1945-1954 section the results were as follows: 8 percent favored increasing the number, 39 percent favored maintaining the same level, 33 percent favored decreasing, and 20 percent had no opinion. The 1965 results did not differ significantly from those reported in the 1945-1955 decade.

Notes

1.   The American Conservative Union. Available through: *http://www.conservative.org/about/history01.asp.* Access Date: October 29, 2008.
2.   John W. Kingdon. 1995. *Agendas, Alternatives, and Public Policies.* Second Edition. New York: Harper Collins College Publishers.
3.   Encarta. Available through: *http://encarta.msn.com/encyclopedia_701843822/Gay_Rights_Movement_in_ the_United_States.html.* Access Date: October 29, 2008.
4.   Pamela Skillings. The Stonewall Riots: New York Stonewall is a Landmark in Gay History. Available through: *http://manhattan.about.com/od/glbtscene/a/stonewallriots.htm.* Access Date: October 29, 2008.
5.   *Encarta.* Available through: *http://encarta.msn.com/encyclopedia_701843822/Gay_Rights_Movement_in_ the_United_States.html.* Access Date: October 29, 2008.
6.   History.com. Available through: *http://www.history.com/this-day-in-history.do?action=tdihArticleYear&id=5132.* Access Date: October 29, 2008.
7.   Feminism and Women's Studies. Available through: *http://feminism.eserver.org/workplace/wages/equal-pay.txt.* Access Date: October 30, 2008.
8.   National Organization for Women. Available through: *http://www.now.org/history/purpos66.html.* Access Date: October 30, 2008.

9.   Infoplease. Available through:
      http://www.infoplease.com/spot/womenstimeline1.html. Access Date: October 30, 2008.

10.   U.S. Supreme Court. Available through:
      http://caselaw.lp.findlaw.com/scripts/getcase.pl?navby=case&court=us&vol=3 81&page=479. Access Date: October 30, 2008.

11.   U.S. Supreme Court. Available through:
      http://caselaw.lp.findlaw.com/scripts/getcase.pl?court=us&vol=405&invol=438. Access Date: November 4, 2008.

12.   Canon, Bradley C; and Charles A. Johnson. 1999. *Judicial Policies: Implementation and Impact*. Second Edition. Washington, DC: CQ Press.

13.   CBC.CA. Available through:
      http://www.cbc.ca/windsor/features/detroit-riot/index.html. Access Date: October 30, 2008.

14.   Watts in Perspective. Available through:
      http://www.tcnj.edu/~blohm3/essay.htm. Access Date: October 30, 2008.

15.   CBC.CA. Available through:
      http://www.cbc.ca/windsor/features/detroit-riot/index.html. Access Date: October 30, 2008.

16.   PBS. Available through:
      http://www.pbs.org/pov/pov2007/revolution67/index.html. Access Date: October 30, 2008.

17.   Michael Kofman. Stokely Carmichael, Rights Leader Who Coined "Black Power," Dies at 57. *The New York Times*. November 16, 1998. Available through:
      http://www.interchange.org/Kwameture/nytimes111698.html. Access Date: October 30, 2008.

18.   MLK Online. Available through:
      http://www.mlkonline.net/holiday.html, Access Date: October 30, 2008.

19.   CBS Evening News. Memories of Robert F. Kennedy: CBS' Jeff Greenfield Worked on RFK'S 1968 Campaign—Now He Shares Remembrances of the Man. June 5, 2008. Available through:
      http://www.cbsnews.com/stories/2008/06/05/eveningnews/main4158341.shtml. Access Date: October 30, 2008.

20.   The Life of Robert F. Kennedy. Available through:
      http://robertkennedy.8m.com/bio.htm. Access Date: October 30, 2008.

21.   Preaching Today.com. Available through:
      http://www.preachingtoday.com/illustrations/article_print.html?id=40617. Access Date: October 30, 2008.

22.   Vietnam War.com. Available through:
      http://www.vietnamwar.com/. Access Date: November 3, 2008.

23.   Mark Barringer. The Anti-War Movement in the United States. Available through:
      http://www.english.uiuc.edu/maps/vietnam/antiwar.html. Access Date: November 3, 2008.

24.   History Central.com. Available through:
      http://www.multied.com/asia/TetOffensive.html. Access Date: November 3, 2008.

25.   U.S. Constitution online. Available through:
      http://www.usconstitution.net/constamnotes.html. Access Date: November 16, 2008.

26.   Vietnam Online. Available through:
      http://www.pbs.org/wgbh/amex/vietnam/trenches/my_lai.html. Access Date: November 3, 2008.

27. Doug Linder. An Introduction to the My Lai Courts-Martial. Available through: *http://www.law.umkc.edu/faculty/projects/ftrials/mylai/Myl_intro.html.* Access Date: November 3, 2008.

28. *Encyclopedia Americana.* Available through: *http://ap.grolier.com/article?assetid=0224340-00.* Access date: November 4, 2008.

29. PBS. Going Back to Chicago. Available through: *http://www.pbs.org/newshour/convention96/retro/chicago.html.* Access Date: November 4, 2008.

30. David C. Hanson. "Four Dead in O-hio-O": The Kent State Massacre. Available through: *http://www.vw.vccs.edu/vwhansd/HIS122/KentState.html.* Access Date: November 4, 2008.

31. U.S. Department of State. Available through: *http://www.state.gov/r/pa/ei/bgn/18902.htm#relations.* Access Date: November 4, 2008.

32. High Beam Encyclopedia. Available through: *http://www.encyclopedia.com/doc/1B1-362602.html.* Access Date: November 4, 2008.

33. Vladislav Zubok. The Soviet Union and détente of the 1970s. *Cold War History* 8(4): 427 – 447.

34. CNN. Available through: *http://www.cnn.com/SPECIALS/cold.war/kbank/profiles/brezhnev/.* Access Date: November 4, 2008.

35. Martin Kelly. What are the Basic Facts about the Watergate Hotel Break In? Available through: *http://americanhistory.about.com/od/watergate/f/watergate1.htm.* Access Date: November 4, 2008.

36. Stanley I. Kutler. 1992. *The Wars of Watergate: The Last Crisis of Richard Nixon.* New York: Norton & Company.

37. Watergate. Available through: *http://www.megaessays.com/viewpaper/46030.html#join.* Access Date: November 4, 2008.

38. *Washington Post.com.* The Watergate Story. Available through: *http://www.washingtonpost.com/wp-srv/politics/special/watergate/.* Access Date: November 4, 2008.

39. *Watergate.info.* Available through: *http://www.watergate.info/.* Access Date: November 4, 2008.

40. BBC. Available through: *http://news.bbc.co.uk/onthisday/hi/witness/july/21/newsid_3058000/3058833.stm.* Access Date: November 4, 2008.

11

The United States between 1975 and 1984: Setting the Stage for Ending the Cold War

The opening year of this decade witnessed the end of American involvement in Vietnam, after draining the American economy, military, and society for almost three decades. The early stages for this conclusion occurred during the presidency of Nixon, who took steps to reduce the American military presence in the country and emphasized the responsibility of the Southern Vietnamese.[1] When fighting resumed shortly after the Paris Accords, and South Vietnam surrendered to the Provisional Revolutionary Government, the United States chose not to interfere.[2] Problems at home, mainly the Watergate scandal and its repercussions, were clearly distracting attention from the Vietnam front, for good or bad.

Jimmy Carter became the thirty-ninth president of the United States in 1977, after defeating President Gerald Ford, in an era of rising energy costs, mounting inflation, and continuing tensions. Given these circumstances, Carter worked hard to combat the continuing economic woes of inflation and unemployment. Unfortunately, by the end of his first term, inflation and interest rates were at near record high, and efforts to reduce them caused a short recession.[3]

The lessons from the Arab boycott during the Yom Kippur war were a fresh memory, and were held responsible by many analysts until today for the recession that kept mounting during the 1970s. As such, Carter designed a national energy policy based on conservation, price decontrol, and new technology.[4] This plan included taxes on gasoline, oil, and natural gas, as well as price controls, while providing incentives for industries to shift to coal.[5] As part of his energy plan, President Carter signed the Department of Energy Organization Act, which created the new federal department, merging the Federal Energy Administration and the Energy

Research and Development Administration, as well as energy-related offices from a number of Federal departments and agencies.[6] He also established the Department of Education in 1979.[7]

Carter belonged to a generation of Southern governors who believed in integration and civil rights. But one of the main events on the civil rights front, arguably the most important during his four-year presidency, came from the Supreme Court, not the executive. This was the 1978 Supreme Court decision in *Regents of University of California v. Bakke.* In this ruling, the Court held that the rigid use of racial quotas violated the equal protection clause of the Fourteenth Amendment. But the Court was split five to four,[8] and the issue was far from resolved on either the societal or the Court level.

In the foreign policy domain, Carter is remembered for a number of achievements. He built full diplomatic relations with China, and completed the negotiations for SALT II. One of his most notable and widely aknowledged achievements is brokering the peace treaty between Egypt and Israel in 1979.[9] This treaty set the stage for peace between the two countries. The more inclusive peace process had to wait until 1991 when the U.S. convinced Israel and the majority of Arab countries to join in the Peace Conference in Madrid. The situation was different this time, and the prospect of a comprehensive and lasting peace in the region was not on the horizon, despite the signing of a peace agreement between Jordan and Israel in 1994.

The final years of Carter in office witnessed two incidents that shaped world politics for years to come. The first was the Iranian revolution in 1979, which deposed the Shah and led to the creation of an Islamic state in the country that was an important ally to the United States since World War II. Before the consolidation of power by followers of *Ayatullah* Khomeini, the revolutionaries were known to come from various political groups, including socialists, communists, and nationalists. But most of these groups shared anti-American sentiments based largely on the intensive American meddling in their country's internal affairs, its support for the authoritarian and brutal rule of the Shah, and its earlier role in defeating the efforts of nationalist and leftist former Prime Minister Muhammed Mossadeq to nationalize the Anglo-Iranian Oil Company (now British Petroleum) and establish national economic autonomy. The CIA, in cooperation with British intelligence, coordinated a successful coup against Prime Minister Mossadeq in 1953, only to be followed three years later with Nasser's successful nationalization of the Suez Canal in Egypt in 1956.

The most profound crisis in Carter's presidency started on November 4, 1979, when Iranian militants stormed the American embassy in Tehran and held several Americans captive. This crisis, which lasted until the release of the last hostage on January 20, 1981, attracted much public attention and concern, and was a factor in Reagan's defeat of Carter in the presidential elections of 1980. Carter preferred a policy of restraint and negotiations to protect the lives of American captives,[10] a posture that the Reagan campaign strongly attacked. Some accounts claim that the Reagan campaign struck a deal with the Iranians to defer the release of the captives until after the elections.

Although this accusation is not confirmed, the complicated relations with Iran were still an important factor in another crisis that the Reagan Administration faced in the following decade—the Iran-Contra Affair, which involved selling arms to Iran in exchange for freeing hostages held by the Iran-supported *Hizbullah* organization in Lebanon and to finance aid to the Contras in Nicaragua against the Cuban-backed Sandinistas. The Iran-Contra affair reflected the difficulty of executive control, the relative ease of hiding information from Congress, and the vagueness of moral standards. The Democratic-controlled Congress had passed three legislative amendments, known as the Boland amendments, between 1982 and 1984, restricting CIA and Department of Defense operations in Nicaragua. News of the scandal revealed the weakness of Congress *vis-à-vis* a determined president.[11]

In the meanwhile, Brezhnev had taken the fatal decision of invading Afghanistan on December 25, 1979 to shore up its Soviet-installed government, a war that lasted for almost ten years and led to extensive destruction and long-term consequences. The United Nations General Assembly passed a resolution that stated the Soviet Union should withdraw its forces from Afghanistan. President Carter withdrew the SALT II agreement from consideration by the United States Senate as a result of the invasion, and the détente effectively came to an end. The United States also imposed a grain embargo on the Soviet Union and boycotted the Moscow Summer Olympics in 1980. Tensions between the United States and the Soviet Union continued up to Brezhnev's death in 1982.[12]

The Reagan Administration, which assumed office in 1981, found this invasion an opportunity to pay back its rival for its role during the devastating Vietnam War. The United States assembled a large international coalition, which included Israel and other Middle Eastern countries, mainly Saudi Arabia and Egypt, in addition to Iran, Pakistan, China, and

Western European countries, to support resistance to the Soviet invasion and the pro-Soviet Afghan government.

It is important here to distinguish between two broad categories of resistance fighters in Afghanistan. The first category included Afghani regional warlords, who conducted the main fighting against the Soviets, and who later fought against one another after the Soviet withdrawal. The second was composed of volunteers from several Arab and Muslim countries, who were attracted by the religious overtones of the war, encouraged by their governments and American support for portraying the war as one between faith and infidelity. Several religious groups augmented this perception. One group of *Mujahideen* was known as the Arab fighters, or the Afghan Arabs. The various bands composing this category were poorly-trained and organized, but some of them were able to gain significant experience in guerilla warfare and other military strategies and tactics.

One of the most important leaders of the Egyptian *Islamic Jihad*, Ayman El-Zawahri, traveled early on to assist with the war effort, after being acquitted of charges of participating in the assassination of Egypt's President Anwar El-Sadat. There, he met Osama bin Laden, a wealthy Saudi who became a prominent organizer and financier of the Arab volunteers. Bin Laden thought about creating *Al-Qaeda* as an organization for the *Mujahideen* after the war. When the two men later decided to join forces, their two organizations, *Islamic Jihad* and *Al-Qaeda*, united to form *Qaedat al-Jihad* (meaning the Base of Jihad—holy war), widely known in the media as simply *Al-Qaeda*. Religion-based militancy was like a genie released from the bottle during Afghanistan. The irony is that this release was facilitated by American support, including military, financial, and even moral support. As later events would show, it was very difficult to put this genie back inside the bottle.

The year 1979 witnessed another alarming event, the Three-Mile Island nuclear accident. The accident took place on March 28, 1979, when the Three Mile Island Unit 2 nuclear power plant near Middletown, Pennsylvania experienced a failure in the secondary, non-nuclear section of the plant, resulting in the release of some radioactive gas. Although the accident did not lead to any deaths or injuries, it brought about sweeping changes involving emergency response planning, reactor operator training, human factors, engineering, radiation protection, and many other areas of nuclear power plant operations. It also caused the U.S. Nuclear Regulatory Commission (NRC) to tighten and heighten its regulatory oversight.[13] There was no substantial overhaul of NRC personnel.[14]

The election of Ronald Reagan as the fortieth president of the United States in 1980 represented a shift in the public mood, and a return to republican vigor after almost a decade and a half of democratic control. When he was reelected in 1984 at age 73, he was, and still is, the oldest president in the nation's history. He was first elected at a time when the people were troubled by inflation and the Iran hostage crisis. Reagan came to office with a promise to reinvigorate the American people and reduce their reliance upon Government.[15] His program, known as the Reagan revolution, opened windows of opportunity for certain groups and closed them for others. Huge military spending and a program for limited government during Reagan's presidency burdened the United States with debts that remained a concern for years to come. His program clearly put the Big Government programs of his predecessors to an end. Despite the costs, Reagan should be remembered for being the president who put an end to the Cold War, based on his conviction that the Soviet Union was not a power to contain, but an enemy to destroy.[16]

Only 69 days after assuming office, Reagan survived an assassination attempt and quickly resumed his work. He obtained legislation to stimulate economic growth, curb inflation, increase employment, and strengthen national defense. His policies focused on cutting taxes and curbing government spending. Although his tax policies eliminated many deductions and exempted millions of people with low incomes,[17] poverty exploded in the inner cities of America during the Reagan years. Programs targeted at low-income families, such as Aid for Families with Dependent Children (AFDC), school lunches, and housing subsidies, were cut back, far more than other programs such as Social Security.[18]

Reagan's Right Wing ideology was also tough on labor, arguably not much different from Thatcher's policies in the United Kingdom. On August 3, 1981, more than 12,000 members of the Professional Air Traffic Controllers Organization organized a strike that would redefine labor relations in America for years to come. In response to the strike, Reagan announced that the controllers were in violation of the law, and that if they did not resume their work in 48 hours, their jobs would be terminated. When the controllers refused to abide, Reagan carried out his threat.[19]

On the women's rights front, Reagan's era witnessed an important achievement. On July 7, 1981, President Reagan nominated Sandra Day O'Connor to the Supreme Court. In September 1981, she became the first female member in the history of the Court.[20] On another account, the House of Representatives passed a bill on August 2, 1983 creating Martin Luther King Day, to be observed on the third Monday in January.

Attempts to establish a national day to honor the civil rights leader started soon after his assassination. The first state to sign a holiday in King's memory was Illinois in 1973, followed by Massachusetts (1974), New Jersey (through a ruling of its Supreme Court—1975). President Reagan signed the bill establishing the national holiday on November 3, 1983. The first national King Holiday was observed on January 20, 1986.[21] It is interesting, and maybe symbolic too, that the inauguration of President Obama took place on this same day of the year 2009.

The discovery of the first case of AIDS in the United States in 1981 was met with mounted fears complicated with limited information. At that time it was perceived as a virus affecting primarily gay men. During the early years of the epidemic, there were limited coordinated efforts by the media and educational institutions to inform the people about the deadly virus. The first national campaign using television and print advertising emerged in the late 1980s.[22]

On the foreign policy front, Reagan planned to pull the Soviet Union into an arms race that would defeat its frail economy. He announced the Star War program, and increased defense spending by 35 percent during his two terms in office.[23] Although his plan was successful in setting the stage for the collapse of the Soviet Union, it proved to be a financial catastrophe for the United States as well. Later, after the end of the Cold War, during the presidency of Bill Clinton, the American government was able to balance the budget, only to lose control again during the presidency of George W. Bush, mainly as a result of military expansion.

On October 25, 1983, the United States invaded Grenada following a bloody coup by Cuban-trained military who executed Prime Minister Maurice Bishop, and at least thirteen of his associates. The act shook the world, and enticed criticism from a number of countries, including Great Britain, a close ally of the United States. The United Nations General Assembly also condemned this act as a violation of international law.[24] On another front, the rise of Mikhail Gorbachev to power in the Soviet Union was soon to change the nature of the Cold War. Concerned with internal problems and economic hardships, Gorbachev sought a policy of cooperation with the United States. But the Reagan Administration was keen not to let the opportunity of putting an end to the Soviet Union go unutilized. Steps toward speeding the Soviet fall were pursued steadily in the United States security establishment.

Reagan also declared war against international terrorism.[25] The U.S. Embassy bombing in Beirut, Lebanon on April 18, 1983 is often referred to as the first terrorist attack conducted by Islamist militants against

American interests. The *Islamic Jihad* group claimed responsibility for the attack.[26]

Public Opinion 1975-1984

African Americans

There were no national survey data from 1975 to 1984 on black/white relations or on attitudes toward African Americans.

Jews

In 1981, a national survey asked respondents to indicate whether they thought the following qualities about Jews were "probably true" or "probably false." They could also answer that they were "not sure."

Beliefs about Jews among Non-Jews in 1981

	(Percent)	
	Probably true	Not sure
Jews are usually hard working people.	81	13
Jews have a strong faith in God.	71	21
Jews are warm and friendly people.	64	26
Jews are just as honest as other businessmen.	60	23

On each of the responses at least 83 percent of the respondents answered "probably true" or "not sure."

The Anti Semitic Index included in a 1981 survey showed the following results.

Statement		1981
1.	Do you think Jews have too much power in the U.S.	23
2.	Do you think Jews have too much power in the business world.	37
3.	Jews are more willing than others to use shady tactics to get what they want.	33
4.	Jews are more loyal to Israel than to America.	48
5.	Jews are not as honest as other businessmen.	22
6.	Jews have a lot of irritating traits.	28
7.	International banking is pretty much controlled by Jews.	43
8.	Jews don't care what happens to anyone but their own kind.	21
9.	Jews always like to be at the head of things.	52
10.	Jews stick together too much.	53
11.	The trouble with Jewish businessmen is that they are so shrewd and tricky other people don't have a chance in competition.	27
	Asked in 1992, 1998, and 2002 instead of #7 "Jews have too much control/influence on Wall St."	

Like the earlier years, items 9 and 10 received the most support.

Gays and Lesbians

When asked in 1977, the first time a question about gays and lesbians was included on a national survey, "Do you think homosexual relations between consenting adults should be or should not be legal?" 43 percent answered "should be legal," 41 percent said "should not be legal" and 14 percent said they had no opinion.

When asked in 1982, 45 percent answered should be legal and 39 percent said should not be legal.

The following questions were also included in polls conducted in 1977.

1.   "As you may know, there has been considerable discussion in the news regarding the rights of homosexual men and women. In general, do you think homosexuals should or should not have equal rights in terms of job opportunities?"
2.   "In your view is homosexuality something a person is born with or is homosexuality due to factors such as upbringing and environment?"

On question 1, 56 percent answered that they should have equal rights in terms of job opportunities and on question 2, 13 percent said that homosexuality is something a person is born with, 56 percent said homosexuality is a function of upbringing and environment, and 14 percent answered "both."

When asked, "Do you feel homosexuality should be considered an acceptable alternative life style or not?" 34 percent answered "acceptable," 51 percent answered "not acceptable" and 15 percent said they had no opinion.

In 1977, we see that the public was evenly divided at 43 percent about whether homosexual relations between consenting adults should be legal. And in 1982, half of the respondents (51 percent) did not believe that homosexuality should be an acceptable alternative life style.

Also in 1977 and 1982 when asked whether "homosexuals should or should not have equal rights in terms of job opportunities," 50 percent answered in the affirmative in 1977 and 59 percent in 1982.

During the same time period, when the public was asked: "In your view is homosexuality something a person is born with or is homosexuality due to factors such as upbringing and environment?"

Fifty-six percent in 1977 and 52 percent in 1982 answered that homosexuality was a function of upbringing and environment; 14 and 13 percent answered "both."

Immigration

Concerning levels of immigration, consistent with earlier years, between 4 and 7 percent favored an increase in immigration but at 65 and 66 percent an even higher percentage favored a decrease in immigration.

In 1982, a national poll stated "Since the beginning of our country people of many different religions, races, and nationalities have come here and settled." Respondents were then asked:

"On the whole do you think they have been a good thing or a bad thing for this country?"

The responses show that immigrants who came earlier are viewed as having been a good thing for this country. But immigrants who are entering the country around the period the question was asked are viewed in a negative light, *i.e.*, Cubans, 59 percent, Haitians and Vietnamese, 39 and 38 percent.

On the basic question asked again in 1977, 1981, and 1982, 7, 5, and 4 percent favored increasing the number of immigrants compared to 42, 65, and 66 percent who supported decreasing the number of immigrants admitted.

Nationality	Good	Bad	Different (in %) (a)
English	66	6	60
Irish	62	7	55
Jews	59	9	50
Germans	57	11	46
Italians	56	10	46
Poles	53	12	41
Japanese	47	18	29
Chinese	44	19	25
Mexicans	25	4	21
Koreans	24	30	-6
Vietnamese	20	38	-18
Haitians	10	39	-29
Cubans	9	59	-50

Source: American Institute of Public Opinion (Storrs: Roper Center, University of Connecticut, 1982).
(a)The two categories not shown are "mixed feelings" and "don't know."

In 1982, the public was asked:

Since the beginning of our country people of many different religions, races, and nationalities have come here and settled. Here is a list of some different groups. Would you read down the list and thinking both of what they have contributed to this country and have gotten from the country, tell me whether you think, on balance, they have been a good thing or a bad thing for this country?

The results showed that the English (at 66 percent, the highest) and immigrants from Southern and Eastern Europe were viewed as having made positive contributions. The Japanese and Chinese were viewed in a more positive than negative light. But nationalities who were currently immigrating to the United States (Mexicans, Koreans, Vietnamese, Haitians, and Cubans) were all viewed negatively.

Abortion

The first national survey that included a question on abortion was conducted in 1974. When asked whether "abortion should be legal under any circumstances" or "illegal in all circumstances," 20 percent answered "yes" to the former and 20 percent answered "yes" to the latter choice.

Notes

1.   History.com. Available through:
      http://www.history.com/encyclopedia.do?articleId=225210. Access Date: November 8, 2008.
2.   The History Place. Available through:
      http://www.historyplace.com/unitedstates/vietnam/index-1969.html. Access Date: November 8, 2008.
3.   The White House. Available through:
      http://www.whitehouse.gov/history/presidents/jc39.html. Access Date: November 8, 2008.
4.   *Op cit.*
5.   Milton R. Copulos. 1977. *Carter's Energy Program*. The Heritage Foundation. Available through:
      http://www.heritage.org/Research/EnergyandEnvironment/bg-3.cfm. Access Date: November 8, 2008.
6.   The U.S. Department of Energy. Available through:
      http://www.energy.gov/news/2315.htm. Access Date: November 8, 2008.
7.   The Cato Institute. *CATO Handbook for Congress: Policy Recommendations for the 108th Congress*. Available through:
      http://www.cato.org/pubs/handbook/hb108/hb108-28.pdf. Access Date: November 8, 2008.
8.   Oyes: The U.S. Supreme Court Media. Available through:
      http://www.oyez.org/cases/1970-1979/1977/1977_76_811/. Access Date: November 9, 2008.
9.   The White House. Available through:
      http://www.whitehouse.gov/history/presidents/jc39.html. Access Date: November 9, 2008.

10. Jimmy Carter Library and Museum. The Hostage Crisis in Iran. Available through: *http://www.jimmycarterlibrary.org/documents/hostages.phtml*. Access Date: November 9, 2008.

11. Julie Wolf. The Iran-Contra Affair. American Experience. Available through: *http://www.pbs.org/wgbh/amex/reagan/peopleevents/pande08.html*. Access Date: November 9, 2008.

12. Glenn E. Curtis, ed. 1996. *Russia: A Country Study*. Washington: GPO for the Library of Congress. Available through: *http://countrystudies.us/russia/*. Access Date: November 9, 2008.

13. U.S. NRC website. Fact Sheet on the Three Mile Island Accident. Available through: *http://www.nrc.gov/reading-rm/doc-collections/fact-sheets/3mile-isle.html*. Access Date: November 9, 2008.

14. American Experience. Available through: *http://www.pbs.org/wgbh/amex/three/peopleevents/pandeAMEX86.html*. Access Date: November 9, 2008.

15. The White House. Available through: *http://www.whitehouse.gov/history/presidents/rr40.html*. Access Date: November 10, 2008.

16. Peggy Noonan. Ronald Reagan: He brought Big Government to its Knees and stared down the Soviet Union. And the audience loved it. *Time*. Available through: *http://www.time.com/time/time100/leaders/profile/reagan.html*. Access Date: November 10, 2008.

17. The White House. Available through: *http://www.whitehouse.gov/history/presidents/rr40.html*. Access Date: November 10, 2008.

18. On the Issues: Every Political Leader on Every Issue. Available through: *http://www.ontheissues.org/Celeb/Ronald_Reagan_Welfare_+_Poverty.htm*. Access Date: November 10, 2008.

19. Kathleen Schalch. 1981 Leaves Legacy for American Workers. NPR. Available through: *http://www.npr.org/templates/story/story.php?storyId=5604656*. Access Date: November 10, 2008.

20. Lucidcafé Library. Available through: *http://www.lucidcafe.com/library/96mar/oconnor.html*. Access Date: November 10, 2008.

21. The King Holiday: A Chronology. Available through: *http://www.thekingcenter.org/holiday/chronology.pdf*. Access Date: November 10, 2008.

22. The Henry A. Kaiser Family Foundation. 2006. Evolution of An Epidemic: 25 Years of HIV AIDS Medcia Campaigns in the U.S. Available through: *http://www.kff.org/entpartnerships/upload/7515.pdf*. Access Date: November 10, 2008.

23. The White House. Available through: *http://www.whitehouse.gov/history/presidents/rr40.html*. Access Date: November 10, 2008.

24. BBC. 1983: U.S. troops invade Grenada. Available through: *http://news.bbc.co.uk/onthisday/hi/dates/stories/october/25/newsid_3207000/3207509.stm*. Access Date: November 10, 2008.

25. *Op cit.*

26.   The Beirut Memorial online. Available through: *http://www.beirut-memorial.org/history/embassy.html*. Access Date: November 10, 2008.

12

The United States between 1985 and 1994: Sunset and Dawn

This decade witnessed the sunset of the Cold War era and huge military spending. By the time the decade reached mid-life, hopes grew for a new world of peace, liberty, and cooperation. These rosy dreams were not only the direct outgrowth of George H. W. Bush's "New World Order," but were reflections of a world society exhausted after years of Cold War tensions and military engagement. The United States benefitted in the post-Cold War era through directing resources away from military spending and toward social policies, balancing the budget, and pushing for more social justice. But Fukuyama's "The End of History" thesis proved a mistake. As usual, history refused to end. Different groups remained with grievances to be answered for, mainly minorities, gays and lesbians, and women. Religion surfaced in new ways to influence the public debate. Arguably a new social movement was growing during this decade, composed mainly of young and more liberal youth, who mirrored the youth movements of the 1960s, but were able to bring a far more revolutionary change than that brought about by the anti-war and leftist movements of the sixties. This change glorified the image of the United States worldwide, and brought hopes that remain to be tested in the years ahead.

As the 1940s and early 1950s witnessed the sunset of the era of European dominance and the dawn of the Cold War, the late 1980s and early 1990s witnessed the sunset of the Cold War and the dawn of the post-Cold War era—although no concrete term has yet been coined to describe the present era. The opening years of this decade did not go without challenges and tensions. On April 15, 1986, President Reagan ordered a series of air strikes against Libya on what the White House called "terrorist centers" and military bases in the country.[1]

The first catastrophe during the decade came with the explosion of the Challenger space shuttle on January 28, 1986, only a few seconds after its launch, killing all seven crew members on board—an incident that shocked the American people.[2] In his remarks about the disaster, President Reagan noted that "we've never had a tragedy like this."[3]

The Challenger disaster was still in the near past when the United States faced an environmental disaster that aroused many concerns. On March 24, 1989, the Exxon Valdez oil tanker hit a reef in Alaska's Prince William Sound resulting in a huge oil spill—close to 30 million gallons. Hundreds of miles of pristine coastline became coated with oil, and thousands of birds, mammals, and fish perished.[4] The spill took four years to clean up.[5]

Another serious environmental catastrophe took place during this decade—the Great Flood of 1993. Few disasters in American history match the devastation caused by this flood, when hundreds of levees along the Mississippi and Missouri Rivers failed, killing 50 people and causing more than $15 billion in damage. Fifty thousand homes were destroyed or damaged and 75 towns were under flood waters. The flood lasted from May through September, occurring across North Dakota, South Dakota, Nebraska, Kansas, Minnesota, Iowa, Missouri, Wisconsin, and Illinois.[6] The inadequacy of the levees and poor preparedness were soon to resurface as a repeated cause for destruction when Hurricane Katrina hit New Orleans in August 2005.

George H. W. Bush, who was President Reagan's Vice President during his second term, was elected president in 1988 during a time of dramatic change. Highlighting the rising opportunities on the international horizon, President Bush pointed out in his Inaugural Address that this was "a moment rich with promise for American power."[7]

On November 9, 1989, the leader of East Berlin's communist party (SED) announced that the border between East and West Germany would be opened for "private trips abroad." On the following day, demolition works on the Berlin wall started, and the fall of the wall was officially announced soon after.[8]

On December 20, 1989, President Bush ordered the dispatch of American troops into Panama to overthrow the regime of General Manuel Antonio Noriega. This was the first use of troops for a cause unrelated to the Cold War since 1945. It was also the first large scale use of troops abroad since Vietnam. Noriega was captured and brought to the United States for trial.[9] The former head of state had been convicted on February 14, 1988 by a federal grand jury in Miami, Florida who returned a twelve-count indictment charging Noriega with participating in an international conspiracy to import cocaine and materials used in producing cocaine into and out of the United States. It became clear that dictators like Noriega, Saddam Hussein, and Slobodan Milošević would remain a challenge in the post-Cold War era.[10]

Another dictator who would make headline news in the following decade is Augosto Pinochet, the Chilean dictator between 1974 and 1990. In 1973, Pinochet led a successful coup supported by the CIA against the democratically elected communist administration of Salvador Allende. Thousand of Chileans were tortured, killed, and disappeared under the regime of Pinochet. By the end of the 1980s, the Reagan Administration became increasingly frustrated by the brutality of the Pinochet regime it helped install and protect. Pressures mounted against the Chilean dictator who was forced to hold a Presidential plebiscite in 1988.[11] Fifty-five percent of the voters rejected him, and he quit the presidency two years later. He remained Commander-in-Chief of the Armed forces and then made himself a senator for life.[12] Pinochet soon became a test to the international community's will and dedication to apply human rights laws to dictators. Although a Spanish judge ordered his arrest on charges of violating human rights and the rule of law, the government of Great Britain, where Pinochet was residing, decided that he was too old to stand trial.[13]

The hopes created by Gorbachev's assumption of power in the Soviet Union, and the impending fall of the Berlin wall, created new challenges. Hope reached Chinese youth, labor activists, and intellectuals, who demonstrated in and near the Tiananmen Square in their country's capital between April 15 and June 4, 1989, calling for democratic reforms. But the Chinese government was not ready for democratic refomers of this sort, and late on June 3, the army moved into the square, randomly firing on unarmed protestors. Several hundred civilians were killed during the bloody military operation. President Bush condemned the use of force.[14] The human rights record of the Chinese government was already an issue of contention in the bilateral relations with the United States. The Tiananmen Square massacre only added fuel to the fire. So far, the economic, political, and strategic relations between the two countries had proven more important for the United States than the human rights record.

The main challenge that faced President Bush, which he was also able to manage with the utmost insight, was the Iraqi invasion of Kuwait on August 2, 1990. The United States had to respond to this invasion for a number of reasons. First, there was the need to establish its leadership in the new era, and make it clear that the new international order would not allow certain actions by states. Second, the invasion represented a threat to oil supplies from the Middle East, in addition to threatening a close American ally—Saudi Arabia. Bush rallied the United Nations, the American people, and Congress behind the cause of freeing Kuwait, and created a broad international coalition against Iraq. After weeks of air and missile bombardment, the 100-hour land battle dubbed Desert Storm routed the Iraqi invasion.[15]

The operation was a success in terms of achieving its goals with minimal losses, in addition to gaining international legitimacy through establishing the United Nations' support. This operation opened the door for initiating the Middle East Peace Process, which despite the hopes at the time, remain far from being concluded. In the aftermath of the Gulf war, the United States cosponsored with the Soviet Union an invitation to Israel, Syria, Lebanon, Jordan and the Palestinian Liberation Organization (PLO) to the Madrid Conference, which set the stage for the Peace talks,[16] resulting so far in only one significant agreement: the Peace Treaty between Jordan and Israel in 1994. The Soviet Union finally collapsed shortly after the conference.

Despite President Bush's foreign policy successes, his domestic policies were criticized as lacking direction, especially in the economic domain. The economic situation was one important factor in setting the stage for his defeat in the 1992 presidential election despite his widespread popularity after the Gulf war. Many of his domestic policy initiatives were pitted against a Congress under democratic control. The federal deficit soared and President Bush had to revise his "no new taxes" pledge during his 1988 campaign. This led to challenges from within his own party. With the seeming lack of vision on the economic front and rising unemployment, the public was ready for a change in the White House.[17]

It is even possible to argue that a change in public mood was spreading worldwide. Margaret Thatcher dominated British politics for eleven years between 1979 and 1990. Together with Ronald Reagan, they both led a coordinated right-wing ideology that embarked on a grand program of privatization, cutting government spending, and advancing free market capitalism. In 1990, she failed to receive the majority vote with a sufficient margin on the ballot for the Conservative leader. She resigned, and John Major succeeded her as party leader and Prime Minister.[18] Soon afterwards, in 1997, Labor Party leader Tony Blair attained the top government position in Great Britain. He was about the same age as

Clinton when he gained power—mid-forties. Discussions of a Third Path between Capitalism and Socialism gained momentum with the rise of these young leaders to power, which was also a reflection of the publics' need to find orientation in the new era.

The civil rights front witnessed an incident that reflected continued tensions despite the achievements of previous decades. Los Angeles experienced intense rioting, the worst since the Watts riots of 1965. As if by a twist of fate, the background story for these riots was not much different from the earlier riots almost three decades ago. Again, it all started when a California highway patrol police stopped a car, this time for exceeding the speed limit (in 1965, the cause was suspicion of drunk driving). After a high-speed chase, the driver, Rodney King, was ordered to exit the vehicle. The police officers started beating him fiercely. The incident was videotaped by an amateur cameraman living nearby, and was soon aired worldwide, sending shockwaves throughout the globe. The riots started a year later, on April 29, 1992, when the four officers accused of beating King were acquitted by a predominantly white jury. The riots, which lasted for six days, left fifty-three people dead and a billion dollars in property damage.[19]

Another Civil Rights-related demonstration occurred in 1990. Anti-discrimination marches, allegations of racism, and mass arrests errupted in Selma, Alabama starting in December. The backdrop for these events was the removal of Norward Roussell from his post as the first black superintendent of schools in a racially-divided decision. Roussell was appointed superintendent by the Selma Board of Education in February 1987. On December 21, 1990, the Board voted not to renew Roussell's three-year contract. The five black members of the Board voted for Roussell, while the six white members voted against him. The reaction was fast and furious, and events soon turned violent.[20]

But the Civil Rights movement also achieved impressive gains during this decade. Edith Erby Jones became the first African American woman president of the National Medical Association in 1985. In 1987, Audrey Borbes Manley became the first African American woman appointed Principal Deputy Assistant Secretary for Health. In 1987, Debora Stith was the first female, African American and youngest-ever Commissioner of Public Health for the Commonwealth of Massachusetts. Vivian Pinn was the first female African American woman Director of the Office of Research on Women's Health at the National Institutes of Health. In 1990, Antonia Novello became the first female and first Latina appointed Surgeon General of the United States. The year 1990 also witnessed Marilyn Gaston becoming the first female and the first African American woman Director of the Bureau of Primary Health Care,[21] and Roselyn Epps becoming the first African American woman to be named president of the American Medical Women's Association. A number of African American men also made significant achievements during this decade. Affirmative action pioneer Arthur Fletcher was named by President George H.W. Bush to chair the United States Commission on Civil Rights. In the same year David Dinkins was sworn in as the first African American Mayor of New York City.[22]

In 1989, Army General Colin Powell became the first black to serve as chairman of the Joint Chiefs of Staff. And in the same year in Virginia, Lawrence Douglas Wilder became the first black elected Governor.[23]

In March 1990, Carole Gist became the first African American to win the title "Miss USA."[24] Later in the same month, Denzel Washington won the Academy Award for Best Actor in a Supporting Role.[25] In November 1990, Charles Johnson, an African American, won the National Book Award for fiction for his novel *Middle Passage*.[26]

In another part of the world, significant and relevant events were taking place. Nelson Mandela, leader of the movement to end apartheid in South Africa, was released from prison on February 11, 1990, after spending 27 years in confinement. Moves toward ending apartheid in South Africa began to accelarate at about the same rate as the Cold War's downfall. When Frederick W. de Klerk became president of South Africa in 1989, the whole ancient regime began to dismantle. Mandela and de Klerk jointly won the Nobel Peace Prize in 1993, and a year later, Mandela became the first elected black president of South Africa.[27]

Amidst these domestic and international developments, it came as a shock when President Bush vetoed the Civil Rights bill in 1990. The bill aimed at job protections that civil rights groups claimed were cut back by recent Supreme Court decisions, especially rulings which made it difficult to prove and win job discrimination lawsuits. It also aimed at banning racial harassment on the job and allow juries to award compensatory and punitive damages in cases of intentional discrimination based on sex and religion. Despite winning majorities in both houses of Congress, the president objected to setting job quotas and insisted on putting a ceiling on compulsory and punitive damages that could be awarded to women and members of religious minorities who were able to prove they were subject to discrimination.[28] He claimed that the bill's "new and very technical rules of litigation" would make it too difficult for employers to defend themselves against charges of discrimination."[29] Clearly this step was detrimental to Bush's quest for a second term in office. As Ronald H. Brown, chairman of the Democratic Party, said, "At the crossroads of his Presidency, George Bush has made clear where he and his Republican Party really stand."[30]

Despite this failure, an important bill was passed during Bush's presidency. This was the Clean Air Act Amendments of 1990. In June 1989, President Bush proposed sweeping revisions to the Clean Air Act. The proposal aimed at curbing three major threats to the environment and public health: acid rain, urban air pollution, and toxic air emissions. The proposal also called for establishing a national system of tradable permits to achieve the desired pollution reductions within nationally specified standards. The bill passed both Houses of Congress by large majorities. This was the last major amendment to the act, but there have been minor changes since then.[31] Despite its success in pollution reduction, the Act polarized free market economists and environmentalists. The former group, based on their conviction that free market values would provide the best solution for environmental problems, perceived emission trading permits as an economically viable and efficient alternative. On the other hand, environmentalists perceived the emissions permits as providing rights to pollute, something which was morally unacceptable and possibly counterproductive.

A significant achievement was also accomplished on the civil rights front in 1990. The Hate Crimes Statistics Act was passed, which requires the Justice Department to acquire data on crimes which "manifest prejudice based on race, religion, sexual orientation, or ethnicity" from law enforcement agencies across the country and to publish an annual summary of the findings. This Act was expanded in 1994 through the Violent Crime Control and Law Enforcement Act, which also required FBI to report on crimes based on "disability."[32]

President Bush signed into law the Americans with Disabilities Act (ADA) in 1990. The Act prohibits private employers, state and local governments, employment agencies and labor unions from discriminating against qualified individuals with disabilities in job application procedures, hiring, firing, advancement, compensation, job training, and other terms, conditions, and privileges of employment. The Act also makes it unlawful to retaliate against an individual for opposing employment practices that discriminate based on disability or for filing a discrimination charge, testifying, or participating in any way in an investigation, proceeding, or litigation under the ADA.[33]

When campaigns for the 1992 presidential elections started, the American public was ripe for change. The Cold War was over; a younger, and more liberal generation was ready for correcting the problems of the past: social injustices, discrimination, and poverty. The then Arkansas Governor, Bill Clinton, and his running mate, Tennessee's Senator Albert Gore Jr., were both in their forties at that time. They represented a new generation of American political leaders eager to answer for the new post-Cold War needs for peace, economic prosperity, and social justice.[34]

Clinton's campaign slogan "It's the economy, stupid!" reflected the need of Americans to get over their economic hardships, huge military spending during the Cold War, and focus on domestic reform. During the Clinton years, the United States enjoyed much-needed peace and economic well-being. He was the first Democratic president since Franklin D. Roosevelt to win a second term. He could point to the lowest unemployment rate in modern times, the lowest inflation in thirty years, the highest home ownership in the country's history, dropping crime rates in many places, and reduced welfare rolls. He proposed the first balanced budget in decades and achieved a budget surplus. As part of a plan to celebrate the millennium in 2000, Clinton called for a great national initiative to end racial discrimination.[35]

Clinton's huge program for health care reform was defeated during his second year in office. He then shifted emphasis toward fulfilling his campaign promise to end big government and create a bureaucracy that "works better and costs less." The National Performance Review, which started in 1993, aimed at creating efficiency, entrepreneurship, and results-focus in the work of the federal government. It is arguably the longest program for Public Administration reform since it lasted, under the direct supervision of the vice president, until the end of Clinton's second term in office in 2000. The early years of the Clinton Administration also witnessed the signing of the North American Free Trade Agreement, NAFTA, in 1993.

Terrorist threats and attempts on U.S. interests even in the homeland were starting to gain momentum during this decade. These threats did not gain much attention at the time, which is probably one reason why after 9/11, President Clinton was accused of having been "soft on terror." The first attempt at the World Trade Center occurred on February 26, 1993 when a car bomb was detonated below Tower One. The intended plan was to knock the North Tower on the South Tower, bringing down both buildings. The attack failed, but led to killing six people and the injury of hundreds of others. Ramzi Youssef, the mastermind and main agent of the attack, was caught and convicted with four other people for carrying out the bombing.[36] The twist of fate was that Khaled Sheikh Mouhammed, Youssef's uncle and a financier of the 1993 bombing, was able to mastermind a success-ful attack on the two towers almost ten years later—on September 11, 2001.

The scientific community during this decade achieved breakthroughs that have changed human life ever since. The release of Windows 95 by the Microsoft Corporation on August 24, 1995 revolutionized the cyber and computer world.[37] The Hubble Space Telescope revolutionized astronomy by providing scientists with the ability to get deep and clear views of the Universe, including not only of our own solar system, but also extremely remote fledgling galaxies. The Telescope was launched in 1990, and was greatly expanded afterwards.[38]

Public Opinion Data 1985-1994

African Americans

There were no items included on national polls between 1975 and 1984 on black/white relations or on attitudes toward African Ameri-cans.

When asked between 1989 through 1994 "Do black children have the same chance as whites to get a good education in your community?" between 80 and 83 percent answered in the affirmative.

And in response to the question of whether blacks have the same chances as whites to get affordable housing in their community, 71 and 74 percent answered "yes" in 1989 and 1991.

Looking into the future in 1986, 57 percent of black respondents thought their future would be better.

Jews

The Anti-Semitic Index items included on a 1992 national survey also showed that items 9 and 10 received the strongest support. But in 1992 about a third of the respondents also thought Jews were more loyal to Israel than to America and Jews have too much power.

Statement	1992
1. Do you think Jews have too much power in the U.S.	31
2. Do you think Jews have too much power in the business world.	24
3. Jews are more willing than others to use shady tactics to get what they want.	21
4. Jews are more loyal to Israel than to America.	35
5. Jews are not as honest as other businessmen.	16
6. Jews have a lot of irritating traits.	22
7. International banking is pretty much controlled by Jews.	Not asked
8. Jews don't care what happens to anyone but their own kind.	16
9. Jews always like to be at the head of things.	39
10. Jews stick together too much.	51
11. The trouble with Jewish businessmen is that they are so shrewd and tricky other people don't have a chance in competition.	19
Asked in 1992, 1998, and 2002 instead of #7 "Jews have too much control/influence on Wall St."	27

Gays and Lesbians

From 1985 through 1992, the question concerning whether homosexual relations between consenting adults should be legal that was asked in the previous decade was included on national polls. Between 1986 and 1988, about one third thought they should be legal. From 1989 through 1992, almost one half, 47 and 48 percent thought they should be legal.

	Should be legal	Should not be legal	No Opinion
1985 Nov 11-18	44	47	9
1986 Jul 11-14	32	57	11
1986 Sep 13-17	33	54	13
1987 Mar 14-18	33	55	12
1988 Jul 1-7	35	57	11
1989 Oct 12-15	47	36	17
1992 Jun 4-8	48	44	8

Additional questions asked in the previous decade that also appeared on national surveys between 1985 and 1994 included whether respondents felt that homosexuality should be considered an acceptable lifestyle to which 38 percent answered acceptable and 57 percent answered not acceptable in 1992. And, whether homosexuals should have equal rights in terms of job opportunities, to which between 71 and 80 percent thought they should.

On whether homosexuality is something a person is born with, or is a function of upbringing and environment, in 1985, 48 percent answered the latter, 19 percent the former, and 12 percent both. In 1989, 60 percent answered "both."

Between October 1989 and April 1993, the percentage of respondents who believed homosexuals should have equal rights "in terms of job opportunities" increased from 71 percent to 80 percent.

Immigration

Consistent with responses in the earlier decades, when asked about levels of immigration between 4 and 9 percent favored increasing immigration from 1985 through 1994 and the majority, between 49 and 54 percent, favored a decrease in immigration.

In 1985 and 1993, the American public was asked whether the following nationalities have "benefitted the country" or "created problems."

Public Opinion on Immigrants by Ethnicity, 1985-1993

Nationality	Benefit Country 1985	Benefit Country 1993	Create Problems 1985	Create Problems 1993	Difference (Benefits-Problems) 1985	Difference (Benefits-Problems) 1993
Irish	78	76	5	11	73	65
Poles	72	65	7	15	65	50
Chinese	69	59	13	31	56	28
Koreans	52	53	23	33	29	20
Vietnamese	47	41	30	46	17	-5
Mexicans	44	29	37	59	7	-30
Haitians	31	19	35	65	-4	-46
Iranians	32	20	40	68	-12	-48
Cubans	29	24	55	64	-26	-40

Source: USA Today/CNN, 1993.

We see that like the responses in the previous decade the immigrants who came earlier are viewed as having benefitted the country as opposed to those who are coming now who are perceived, especially in 1993, as creating problems.

Abortion

In May 1987 and May 1993, the public was asked: "Do you favor or oppose making it more difficult for a woman to get an abortion?"

In 1987, 51 percent opposed making it more difficult and in 1993, 60 percent said they opposed making it more difficult. When respondents were divided by religions, Jews and Agnostics at 87 and 76 percent were most likely to oppose making it more difficult. Only a majority of white Evangelical Protestants (56 percent) favored making it more difficult. Only 36 percent of the Catholic respondents favored making it more difficult for a woman to get an abortion.

And when asked in March 1993, "Should abortion be generally available, available with stricter limits, not available?" the results looked like this:

	Percent
Generally Available	42
Available but with Stricter Limits	36
Not Available	24

Notes

1.   Bernard Weinraub. 1986. U.S. Jets Hit 'Terrorist Centers' in Libya; Reagan Warns of New Attacks if Needed. The *New York Times*. April 15. Available through: *http://www.nytimes.com/1986/04/15/politics/15REAG.html*. Access Date: November 10, 2008.

2.   BBC. 1986: Seven dead in space shuttle disaster. Available through: *http://news.bbc.co.uk/onthisday/hi/dates/stories/january/28/newsid_2506000/2506161.stm*. Access Date: November 16, 2008.

3.   Ronald Reagan remarks on the Challenger Shuttle explosion. Available on YouTube through:
http://video.google.com/videosearch?hl=en&q=challenger+shuttle+disaster&um=1&ie=UTF-8&sa=X&oi=video_result_group&resnum=4&ct=title#. Access Date: November 16, 2008.

4.   History.com. Available through:
http://www.history.com/this-day-in-history.do?action=Article&id=382. Access Date: November 16, 2008.

5.   BBC News. Oil tanker runs aground in Alaska. February 2, 2006. Available through: *http://news.bbc.co.uk/2/hi/americas/4675464.stm*. Access Date: November 17, 2008.

6.   Robert Roy Britt. History Repeats Itself: The Great Flood of 1993. *Live Science.* Available through: *http://www.livescience.com/environment/080622-great-flood-1993.html*. Access Date: November 19, 2008.

7.   The White House. Available through: *http://www.whitehouse.gov/history/presidents/gb41.html*. Access Date: November 17, 2008.

8.   The Berlin Wall. Available through: *http://userpage.chemie.fu-berlin.de/BIW/wall.html#demolition*. Access Date: November 17, 2008.

9.   Eytan Gilboa. 1996. The Panama Invasion Revisited: Lessons for the Use of Force in the Post Cold War Era. *Political Science Quarterly* 110(4): 539-562. Winter 1995-1996.

10. The United States v. Noriega Case. Available through: *http://www.gwu.edu/~jaysmith/Noriega.html*. Access Date: November 17, 2008.

11. NPR. Augosto Pinochet: Villain to Some, Hero to Others. Available through: *http://www.npr.org/templates/story/story.php?storyId=6607702*. Access Date: November 19, 2008.

12. Arab News. Available through: *http://www.arabnews.com/?page=7&section=0&article=89907&d=12&m=12&y=2006*. Access Date: November 19, 2008.

13. NPR. Augosto Pinochet: Villain to Some, Hero to Others. Available through: *http://www.npr.org/templates/story/story.php?storyId=6607702*. Access Date: November 19, 2008.

14. BBC Home. 1989: Massacre in Tiananmen Square. Available through: *http://news.bbc.co.uk/onthisday/hi/dates/stories/june/4/newsid_2496000/2496277.stm*. Access Date: November 17, 2008.

15. The White House. Available through: *http://www.whitehouse.gov/history/presidents/gb41.html*. Access Date: November 17, 2008.

16. Palestine Facts. Available through: *http://www.palestinefacts.org/pf_1991to_now_madrid_desc.php*. Access Date: November 17, 2008.

17. American Experience. Available through: *http://www.pbs.org/wgbh/amex/presidents/41_g_h_w_bush/index.html*. Access Date: November 17, 2008.

18. History.com. November 22, 1990: Margaret Thatcher resigns. Available through: *http://www.history.com/this-day-in-history.do?action=tdihArticleCategory&id=5541*. Access Date: November 18, 2008.

19. *Time*, in partnership With CNN. The L.A. Riots: 15 Years after Rodney King. Available through: *http://www.time.com/time/specials/2007/la_riot/article/0,28804,1614117_1614084,00.html*. Access Date: November 17, 2008.

20. *People*. In Selma, Ala., Marchers Again Take to the Streets. Available through: *http://www.mikemason.net/work/magazines.php?cat=news&id=6*. Access Date: November 19, 2008.

21. Women of Color. Available through: *http://www.mfdp.med.harvard.edu/woc/timeline/index.htm*. Access Date: November 19, 2008.

22. The History Makers. Available through:
    http://thehistorymakers.com/timeline/index.asp?year=1990&Category=. Access
    Date: November 19, 2008.
23. CNN Interactive. Available through:
    http://www.cnn.com/EVENTS/1997/mlk/links.html. Access Date: November 19,
    2008.
24. Wikipedia. Available through:
    http://en.wikipedia.org/wiki/Carole_Gist. Access Date: November 19, 2008.
25. The History Makers. Available through:
    http://thehistorymakers.com/timeline/index.asp?year=1990&Category=. Access
    Date: November 19, 2008.
26. University of Washington. Available through:
    http://www.washington.edu/research/showcase/1977a.html. Access Date: November 19, 2008.
27. History.com. Available through:
    http://www.history.com/this-day-in-history.do?action=Article&id=4758. Access
    Date: November 19, 2008.
28. Steven Holmes. 1990. President Vetoes Bill on Job Rights; Showdown is Set. The
    New York Times. October 23. Available through:
    *http://query.nytimes.com/gst/fullpage.html?res=9C0CE3D9103DF930A1575
    3C1A966958260&sec=&spon=&pagewanted=1*. Access Date: November 19,
    2008.
29. Tom Wicker. President for a Veto. *New York Times*. Available through:
    *http://query.nytimes.com/gst/fullpage.html?res=9C0CE7D7153DF937A15753
    C1A966958260&scp=91&sq=Bush+civil+rights+veto&st=nyt*. Access Date:
    November 19, 2008.
30. Steven Holmes. 1990. President Vetoes Bill on Job Rights; Showdown is Set. The
    New York Times. October 23. Available through:
    *http://query.nytimes.com/gst/fullpage.html?res=9C0CE3D9103DF930A1575
    3C1A966958260&sec=&spon=&pagewanted=1*. Access Date: November 19,
    2008.
31. U.S. Environmental Protection Agency. Overview: The Clean Air Act Amendments
    of 1990. Available through:
    http://www.epa.gov/air/caa/overview.txt. Access Date: November 19, 2008.
32. The Hate Crimes Statistics Act. Available through:
    http://www.adl.org/issue_government/hate_crime_statistics_act.asp. Access Date:
    November 19, 2008.
33. The U.S. Equal Employment Opportunity Commission. Facts About the Americans
    with Disabilities Act. Available through:
    http://www.eeoc.gov/facts/fs-ada.html. Access Date: November 19, 2008.
34. The White House. Available through:
    http://www.whitehouse.gov/history/presidents/bc42.html. Access Date: November
    17, 2008.
35. *Op cit.*
36. Wikipedia: The Free Encyclopedia. Available through:
    http://en.wikipedia.org/wiki/World_Trade_Center_bombing. Access Date: November 19, 2008.
37. Wikipedia: The Free Encyclopedia. Available through:
    http://en.wikipedia.org/wiki/Windows_95. Access Date: November 19, 2008.
38. National Aeronautics and Space Administration. The Hubble Space Telescope.
    Available through:
    http://hubble.nasa.gov/. Access Date: November 19, 2008.

13

The United States between 1995 and 2004: Enemy Found but Not Defined

The post-Cold War era witnessed an intensive search for direction. As explained in the previous chapter, young and energetic leaders in the United States and Europe attempted to formulate a new Third Way ideology to give hope and opportunities to their societies that were exhausted after years of East-West confrontations. Equal rights for homosexuals and minorities, economic reform, and social spending surfaced highly on the campaign agenda of President Clinton. Human rights violations, including those in foreign countries, also gained attention from the Clinton Administration in addition to its domestic agenda. Humanitarian intervention appeared to be a new mission for the United States in the post-Cold War era, an approach that was not highly welcomed abroad or among a significant segment of the American people.

Under the umbrella of protecting human rights and enforcing peace, NATO interfered to enforce the Dayton Peace treaty, which ended the civil war in former Yugoslavia, a war that lasted from 1992 to 1995, claiming thousands of innocent lives and introducing unprecedented crimes and atrocities by Serbia and Bosnian Serbs against the Muslim population in Bosnia and Herzegovina. American troops constituted one third of the 60,000 NATO troops who were deployed to the country.[1] This operation gained international legitimacy when the U.N. Security Council voted unanimously to authorize NATO to send troops to Bosnia.[2] The contested province of Kosovo remained a source of tension, and the NATO intervention in 1999 aroused international suspicion that the United States was attempting to establish new international norms that allow military intervention on humanitarian grounds, thus replacing the national sovereignty and non-interference principles, which were codified in the UN Charter as the established basis for the international order.

Neglecting the UN cover in moving toward ending the conflict in Kosovo was an alarming step in transcending international legitimacy, only to be dwarfed almost four years later when the United States invaded Iraq in 2003 amidst widespread international opposition.

The backdrop of the Kosovo air bombing campaign by NATO in 1999 was the continued brutality of Serbian President Slobodan Miloševi to counter separatist trends among the Kosovars, and his rejection of the Rambouillet peace agreement.[3] As will be explained later, domestic problems associated with the Monica Lewinsky case were speculated to have had a role in President Clinton's decision to interfere. The bombing campaign ended with the United Nations and NATO assuming almost full responsibility for Kosovo's security. Agitation for independence continued after the NATO operations,[4] and the United States finally recognized Kosovo's independence in 2008.[5]

These interventions came after the United States' disastrous involvement in Somalia, which ended in 1994. President Bush had announced Operation Restore Hope on December 4, 1992 through the United States-led Unified Task Force (UNITAF).[6] The American intervention exacerbated the conflict by pitting warlords against each other. U.S. troops withdrew from Somalia in May 1994 followed by UN forces in March 1995.[7] The deaths and casualties among American soldiers, although limited by conventional war standards, were not expected. Nineteen American soldiers were killed and several dozens were injured.[8] The main shift in American public opinion occurred after airing a video of dead American soldiers dragged through the streets of Mogadishu by crowds in October 1993. President Clinton ordered the termination of all American military operations in the country shortly thereafter.[9]

This tragic intervention deterred the Clinton administration from direct involvement in other failed countries in Africa. His administration therefore chose not to directly intervene when the Rwandan genocide started in 1994. Somalia is one example of a failed state that would continue to cause problems and threats for years to come. Central authority in the country had collapsed in 1991, and since that time the country entered into a state of disarray. Until today, the country is prone to chronic humanitarian emergencies. The UN and the World Bank classify Somalia as a least-developed, low-income country and one of the most food insecure countries in the world.[10]

Given such conditions, and especially given the stratgic location of Somalia on the Gulf of Aden and the Indian Ocean, the country became a place of primary choice for terrorists. But the country also became a safe haven for other international criminal activities as well. International piracy was a recent development that surfaced in 2008. The practice has been common since lawlessness hit hard on the poor African country, but it started rising to an alarming extent when a Ukrainian vessel laden with arms was hijacked by pirates off the coast of Somalia on November 25, 2008. This incident was especially alarming since it aroused fears that the pirates might supply such arms to terrorists.[11] On November 29, 2008, another Liberian tanker carrying chemical materials was also hijacked in the Gulf of Aden.[12] International efforts are building against these new threats, and it will continue to be a test for the readiness of the international community to unite against the threats of terrorism and other rising crimes on the international scene.

These foreign policy issues were not directly affiliated with Clinton's legacy probably until the terrorist attacks of 9/11. His accomplishments on the domestic arena were impressive and brought much hope to the American people. Aside from building on the opportunities that became available after the end of the Cold War, basically through reducing military spending and balancing the budget after decades of deficit, Clinton's record on gay and lesbian rights represented a clear development, although not without criticisms.

In 1994, as part of the Crime Act, President Clinton signed the Hate Crimes Sentencing Enhancement Act, providing for longer sentences where the offense is determined to be a hate crime based on sexual orientation. He issued an Executive Order prohibiting discrimination based on sexual orientation in the Federal civilian workforce, and another Executive Order mandating that security clearances no longer be denied based on sexual orientation. On October 6, 1997, President Clinton appointed James C. Hormel as the U.S. Ambassador to Luxemburg; he was the first openly gay ambassador in American diplomacy.[13] President Clinton also announced his sponsorship of the Hate Crimes Prevention Act, which expands the definition of hate crimes, and used much presidential leverage to pass this bill. The whole issue of homosexuals' rights had been given a boost in October 1998 when Matthew Shepard, a twenty-one-year old gay college student, was robbed and beaten to death. National news shrieked that Shepard was a victim of a hate crime.[14] The Clinton-Gore Administration also attempted to fight discrimination against people with AIDS and increased resources to fight the deadly syndrome, both domestically and internationally, as well as funds for education and prevention.

Opening homosexuality in the military was one of Clinton's campaign promises. The president's decision to permit homosexuals into the army, reversing a 150-year old practice, was definitely revolutionary, although it was also criticized as half-hearted.[15] The new laws and regulations pertaining to homosexuals in the military, issued in 1993, reflected a compromise colloquially referred to as "don't ask, don't tell." This phrase means that service members should not be asked about nor allowed to discuss their homosexuality. Paradoxically, while discharges from the military based on homosexuality were already decreasing until 1993, they increased following the new laws and regulations. Following the Supreme Court's ruling in *Bowers v. Hardwick*, which stipulated that there was no fundamental right to engage in homosexual practices, the courts have uniformly held that the military can discharge a service member for overt homosexual conduct. However, the legal picture became complicated after the Court's 2003 decision in *Lawrence v. Texas* that declared unconstitutional a Texas law that prohibited sexual acts between same-sex couples. In addition to the contradictions on the legal scene, problems of definitions, such as the definition of "sexual orientation" remained paramount.[16] The issue of gay rights in the army gained special attention in 1999 with the murder of gay soldier Barry Winchell by one of his colleagues. The crime was portrayed as based on the slain soldier's sexual orientation.[17]

One of President Clinton's widely acknowledged accomplishments was welfare reform, which reflected his campaign promise to "end welfare as we know it." His plan came at a time when there was an agreement that something should be done regarding this issue. Conservatives criticized welfare given its financial burdens and arguable negative effects on labor supply. Liberals wanted better targeting of welfare to those who need it and better opportunities for the poor to develop their skills and become functional in the society. Federal reforms of the welfare system had stressed the importance of work and employment for recipients of cash assistance. A number of states pioneered the movement toward employment-focused welfare reform programs. Wisconsin, for example, adopted an ambitious experiment in which welfare benefits were largely replaced by private- or public-sector employment. The welfare reform of 1996 took concrete steps toward changing the organizing principles and goals of the welfare system from the provision of cash assistance to the promotion of employment and the reduction of welfare reliance. The most important change was the elimination of federal entitlements for cash assistance and the imposition of a time limit on assistance.[18] The Act gave states incentives to create jobs for people on welfare.[19]

But the new system raised a number of concerns. The old system was criticized for granting benefits to people who did not deserve them. The new system created the possibility that people who deserve welfare might not receive it. Because most public assistance goes to families, many of the victims would inevitably be children. The issue of fairness was also a main consideration. Under the old system, standardization, for all its drawbacks, ensured a certain kind of blind fairness. With much discretion given to welfare workers, there are fears that certain groups, like minorities and people with drug problems, could be treated unfairly. Liberals also criticized the bill for stripping disability and health benefits from legal immigrants.[20] Another main concern with welfare reform was legal. Devolution and the great increase in the reliance on private and non-profit contractors raised fears that legal protections and due process rights embedded in the Constitution might not be extended to citizens receiving public benefits through private contractors. This issue remains an ongoing concern.[21]

With regard to affirmative action, the Supreme Court, which had so far been supportive of affirmative action programs, started to take a more conservative path through applying the standard of "strict scrutiny." In 1995, in *Adarand v. Pena*, the Court ruled in a 5 to 4 decision that any racial classification in affirmative action programs must serve a compelling governmental interest and be narrowly tailored to observe that interest.[22]

On January 25, 1995, the trial of O. J Simpson, the former black football superstar, started on charges that he had killed his white ex-wife and her friend. The trial was one of the most famous trials in American history. It cost millions of dollars, and divided the American society as well as the jury involved on racial lines. The evidence against Simpson was strong, including previous abuse of his wife and DNA analysis that found his blood at the crime scene. But Simpson's defense team was able to plant the seeds of doubt with regards to the evidence available and witnesses' reports. Racial bias was a factor used in these attempts by the defense, which led to a hot societal debate around the Court's procedures. On October 3, 1995, the Jury found Simpson not guilty of the two counts of murder. On December 20, 1996, Simpson was awarded custody of his children by an Orange County judge.[23]

In 1996, the world witnessed an important scientific breakthrough that expectedly pitted religion against science, as has often happened throughout the history of science. Dolly, a Scottish sheep, was born on July 5 of that year, but it was no ordinary sheep. She was a clone, an exact genetic replica of her donor "mother," a six-year-old female sheep. Together with another announcement that scientists in Oregon had cloned monkeys from embryonic cells, an ongoing debate among research- ers, ethicists, and politicians intensified all over the world.[24] Stem cell research remains a hotly debated issue in the United States that divides the political landscape. Congress had banned the use of federal funds for any experiment that creates or destroys a human embryo. The House has twice passed legislation that would outlaw all forms of cloning—in 2001 and again in 2003. But this legislation stalled in the Senate. In 2001 President Bush extended the ban to cover all human embryonic stem cells—making an exception only for certain cells that had already been created by the time of his announcement.[25]

Despite his domestic accomplishments on the economic and social fronts, Clinton was on his way to facing one of the most embarrassing scandals for an American president. That was the Monica Lewinsky case, or the Monicagate, as it was sometimes referred to in the media, after the Watergate scandal, which led to the resignation of President Nixon. The sexual misconduct of the president was an issue since he was Governor of Arkansas. Monica Lewinsky was a White House intern when she had a "sexual relationship" with the president for almost two years between 1995 and 1997. The affair surfaced during legal proceedings connected to his relation with Arkansas state employee Paula Jones. Jones's lawyers sought corroborating evidence of Clinton's conduct to substantiate her allegations against the president during his governorship.

Clearly this case was a golden opportunity for Clinton's domestic rivals. On January 26, 1998, Clinton lied under oath. He famously de- clared that he "did not have sexual relations with that woman." When the presence of invincible evidence was declared, in the form of Monica's blue dress that had the president's DNA on it, Clinton had to admit that he did have some sort of a sexual relationship with Lewinski. Clinton defended his position later by arguing that there was a problem of defini- tion regarding "sexual relationship," and that no relationship existed at the time when he gave his testimony under oath.

Despite being acquitted of all charges and saved an impeachment, the scandal had its imprints on the following two years of the president in office, and weakened his ability to support his vice president, Al Gore, in his quest for the White House in the 2000 presidential race. The scan- dal also discredited many of President Clinton's foreign policy actions. Clinton ordered a series of military strikes against Iraq in December 1998 arguing that Saddam Hussein should not be allowed to threaten his own people and neighbors with weapons of mass destruction. Dubbed Operation Desert Fox, the strikes were a series of strong and sustained attacks.[26] Escalation on the Iraq front was quickly attributed to problems at home, with the possibility that Clinton was distracting public opinion away from his own scandal toward the outside enemy, or that he himself was detracted from being able to prepare a well-crafted strategy for the U.S. policy on Iraq.[27] The bombing started the day before the voting on impeachment and continued throughout the days of the vote.[28]

It was simply impossible for any observer to disentangle the politics of foreign policy from the politics of scandal. The relation between Saddam Hussein's regime and UNSCOM, the United Nations Commission established in 1991 to inspect and dismantle Iraq's non-conventional weapons arsenal,[29] became more tense. The UN Security Council issued a number of resolutions condemning the Iraqi actions regarding weapons' inspections and demanded that it cooperate fully with the Special Commission.[30] Finally, in November 1998, UNSCOM decided to withdraw its remaining staff from Iraq and the United States started its operations shortly afterwards.[31] This decision attracted wide international and domestic criticism given the weak presidential credibility, the refusal of unilateral action, and the fact that many civilians were killed or injured in this campaign. Another critical issue with the choice of timing was that it started during the Muslim holy month of Ramadan, something that fueled antagonism everywhere, especially among Muslims. Sentiments had been fueling with rejection since Clinton, throughout his presidency, insisted on maintaining the sanctions against Iraq, which started after the second Gulf War ended in 1991. A number of religious groups and organizations had condemned the sanctions, including major Christian organizations in the United States.

The deteriorating humanitarian situation in Iraq had invoked the United Nations Security Council to adopt the Oil-for-Food Program in 1995, in which Iraq was allowed to sell part of its oil in order to purchase necessary food and drug items. After delays, humanitarian supplies began to arrive in 1997. The program lessened the crisis, but did not end it. The United States and Great Britain often blocked legitimate humanitarian contracts, claiming that they had "dual use" as military items. Both countries intervened in ways that led to drastically reducing the funds available for the program.[32] The program however was plagued by a scandal in which members of the United Nations staff, private business managers in Europe and the United States, as well as politicians from a number of countries were involved. The allegation was that the regime of Saddam Hussein used oil smuggling and systematic thievery, and demanded illegal payments and kickbacks. According to a 2004 Central Intelligence Agency investigation, Hussein allegedly earned some $1.7 billion through kickbacks and surcharges, and $10.9 billion through illegal oil smuggling.[33]

Elsewhere in the world, in the caves of Afghanistan, conspiracies were taking place. Osama bin Laden and Ayman El-Zawahri, who had met earlier during resistance to the Soviet invasion of Afghanistan, were also in the process of finding new direction and fighting their common enemy—the United States. It is important to note that, although the United States channeled resources for the purpose of defeating the Soviet Union in Afghanistan and draining its rival's power, and although the *Mujahideen* originally joined forces against the Soviets, the United States had always been their primary enemy. Many of their ideas were shaped by the writings of Sayyid Qutb (1906-1966), the Egyptian intellectual who spent two years studying in the United States but was highly critical of its system, and preached *Shari'a* law and violence against the unjust ruler. With the end of the war in Afghanistan, and the settlement of some power disputes among the Afghan Arabs, the two men agreed to unite forces in what they called "The International Front for Fighting the Jews and Crusaders." Ironically, the two men, and their united organizational front, *Qaedat Al-Jihad*, found sanctuary under the rule of Taliban in Afghanistan, who gained control in 1996 with tacit support from Saudi Arabia and the United States. The Saudis and Americans wanted to restore stability to the country after its warlords started fighting following the Soviet withdrawal and the toppling of the Soviet-installed Communist government.

While news of the new alliance and declared front were drawing considerable attention in the American Administration and security establishment, terrorism struck early and quickly. One of Bin Laden's main goals was to drive out the "non-believers" from the holy lands in Saudi Arabia. In November 1995, a car exploded in the Saudi capital, Riyadh, killing five Americans. In June 1996, terrorists attacked the American military complex at Khobar Towers killing nineteen Americans and wounding hundreds more.[34] The bombings were a huge shock in a country that had been a stable and long-term ally of the United States. However, this was only the beginning, and other attacks were soon to follow.

Nearly-simultaneous bombing attacks on the U.S. Embassies in Nairobi, Kenya and Dar es Salaam, Tanzania took place on August 7, 1998. In Nairobi, the attack killed 291 persons and wounded about 5,000. In

Dar es Salaam 10 persons were killed and 77 wounded. Preparations for this attack by Al-Qaeda operatives had started as early as 1993.[35] In retaliation for the attack, American cruise missiles pounded sites in Afghanistan and Sudan on August 20, 1998. The bombing killed 21 and injured 30 in Afghanistan. In the Sudanese capital, Khartoum, a pharmaceutical factory was heavily damaged. American officials argued that it had ties with Bin Laden and was used to produce chemical weapons.[36] Again this time, and despite widespread support for immediate and tough retaliation, critics at home questioned whether Clinton had ordered the bombings to deflect attention from his personal problems.[37] Bombing a pharmaceutical firm also raised widespread protest in a number of Muslim countries, especially in the Middle East.

Al-Qaeda remained determined to strike again. On October 12, 2000, the U.S. Navy destroyer Cole was attacked by a small boat laden with explosives during a brief refueling stop in the harbor of Aden, Yemen. The suicide attack killed 17 crew members and injured 39 others, and almost sunk the ship.[38] American counterintelligence officials found clear similarities between the USS Cole bombings and the earlier bombings in Kenya and Tanzania.[39] Apparently *Al-Qaeda* had developed a trademark that became difficult to mistake.

During the last days of his Presidency, President Clinton aimed at mediating a final peace settlement in the Middle East. Again, skeptics argued that the purpose was to create a legacy for himself that would surpass his scandalous sexual behavior. The argument went on to claim that probably another goal of the president was to win a Nobel Prize—a much needed accomplishment in light of his domestic problems and loss of credibility. Whatever the reasons were, Clinton brought the Israeli Prime Minister Ehud Barak together with PLO Chief Yasser Arafat in Camp David in July 2000 to discuss a final settlement to the Israeli-Palestinian conflict. Although the direct involvement of the American president has often been perceived as a necessity for achieving peace in the region, this involvement had come a bit too late. Distrust between the two parties was high, and animosity was clear. There was little chance that the two-week negotiations in the same place where Sadat and Begin reached agreement under President Carter's sponsorship more than twenty years earlier would lead to anything this time.

The two parties went back home, and each side accused the other of responsibility for the failure of the negotiations. The Palestinians insisted on the full implementation of UN Security Council Resolution 242, arguing that it requires Israel to withdraw from all lands occupied on June 5,

1967, including East Jerusalem. The Israelis argued that the Palestinians, as they had always done, lost a golden opportunity to achieve peace and gain part of their national rights, including limited sovereignty over parts of East Jerusalem. Barak and Arafat were received differently at home. Barak was faced by mounting criticisms and accusations of being ready to give up valuable Jewish land. Arafat was greeted as a hero given his insistence on holding to the full rights of the Palestinian people. The situation was ready for eruption; only a match was needed to incite fire in the Middle East.

The match was ready in the hands of Ariel Sharon, leader of the opposition Likud Party. On September 28, 2000, under heavy guard, Sharon entered the compound around Al-Aqsa Mosque, one of the holiest Muslim sites. News of this event spread like wildfire, and demonstrations started soon after. Palestinians and the Israeli police clashed in the worst violence in several years, which kept escalating for years to come.[40] Violence developed into what became known as the *Second Al-Aqsa Intifada* (uprising), in reference to the first *Intifada* which lasted from 1987 to1993. While the first *Intifada* was not violent on the Palestinian side, the second *Intifada* became highly militarized, with a wave of suicide bombings, referred to in the Arab media as Martyrhood Operations. When the events of September 11 took place almost a year after Sharon's visit, the link between these events and the Palestinian military activities was highlighted by Israeli media everywhere. By that time, Sharon had become Israel's Prime Minister, and a close ally of President Bush.

The presidential elections in 2000 were probably the most controversial and legally (as distinct from politically) contested in the nation's history. The five-week confrontation over vote counting and other irregularities in Florida highlighted not only systematic shortcomings but also central national divisions especially regarding race. The controversy centered on some technical issues with the punch cards, which arguably confused the voters and thus led them to misrepresent their choices. Racial issues included reports that some African Americans were denied the right to vote because their names were incorrectly removed from the official lists of eligible voters or their voter registration applications were not processed correctly. Others were discouraged from voting because of long lines or unhelpful election officials. In addition, some people claimed that many voting machines in predominately African American precincts were old and did not function properly. A computer analysis of the voting by the *Washington Post* indicated that percentages of spoiled ballots were higher in those African American precincts.[41]

On November 9, the Gore campaign asked election officials for hand recounts in four counties in Florida. The Bush campaign asked a federal court in Miami to block the recounts, arguing that manual recounts were unfair because they used a subjective standard unlike the automated machine recounts. The Court refused to block the recount, but Florida's Secretary of State Katherine Harris, a republican and supporter of Bush, refused to extend the November 14 deadline to declare the results. A circuit judge refused to block Harris's decision, and the Gore campaign resorted to the Florida Supreme Court, which ruled unanimously for Gore and ordered an extension of manual recounts until November 26. The Bush campaign quickly appealed to the U.S. Supreme Court, which agreed to hear the case in early December. Chaos in the recounts, especially in the Miami-Dade recount, and court battles continued until December 12, when the Supreme Court effectively ended the 2000 presidential elections. By a vote of 5 to 4, it ruled that there would be no further recounting. The Court split along partisan lines.[42]

In his concession speech, Gore commented on the Supreme Court's decision saying, "While I strongly disagree with the Court's decision, I accept it." The relevant experience derived from these elections is that it highlighted that, despite the nation's progress on human rights, equality, and democracy, there were still unheard voices, structural discrimination, and barriers to social mobility. As Gore said, "Some have asked whether I have any regrets, and I do have some regret. That I didn't get the chance to stay and fight for the American people over the next four years, especially for those who need burdens lifted and barriers removed, especially for those who feel their voices have not been heard."[43]

Putting the elections process aside, the election of George W. Bush was received with caution, especially across the Atlantic. The Europeans were concerned with the rise of the Neo- Conservatives in the Bush Administration. The Neocons started in the Democratic Party, then shifted their efforts to working in the Republican Party. They also shifted toward more concern with foreign policy, and had a high moral tone to their arguments and a preference for independent action. These orientations alerted not just the Europeans, but other governments as well. Although the Bush campaign focused on domestic issues, especially reducing taxes on business, cutting government spending, and reforming social security, foreign policy remained a concern for those who did not want to see the United States acting as a global policeman. During the previous decade, the Neocons had been developing their ideas and plans mainly through research centers and think tanks such as the American Enterprise

Institute. These plans were waiting for the right time to be used, and the right time was approaching. The enemy was preparing to strike, wearing the Islamic cloak.

The terrorist attacks on September 11, 2001 came as a shock to the whole world, even to the U.S. Administration and security apparatus, which already had information about an impending attack by *Al-Qaeda* operatives inside the United States. Americans were shocked by the fact that, for the first time in their history, the enemy was striking on their own land, which was thought to be protected and even isolated from the rest of the world by two oceans. After more than half a century of thinking in terms of the Soviet threat, which in part led President Bush to speak about reviving the Star Wars Program to interdict and destroy any missiles fired at American land, the threat now came through the least expected way—hijacked airplanes. Talks about a missile defense system did not completely disappear, thus maintaining a source of tension with Russia. However, it was clear that the new real threats are more likely to arrive in the form of a small boat full of nuclear explosions than through an Inter-Continental Ballistic missile. Despite the tragedy, the events united a nation that was heavily divided by the recent memory of the 2000 elections.

President Bush acted quickly to restore unity and confidence to the nation. The president was also quick to point out that the war was not against Islam, but rather against terrorism. However, the rise of terms such as "Islamo-fascism" and the intensification of anti-Muslim sentiments in the United States, especially directly after the attacks, were all too clear. The 9/11 Commission report pointed to deadly failures on the part of the Administration as well as the security apparatus. It was clear that the United States was not ready for the new enemy, and the problem of defining this enemy haunted the response.

Al-Qaeda was vague regarding its responsibility for the attacks, only to confirm this responsibility later through video appearances of Bin Laden and Al-Zawahry, which became common occurrences later on. On October 7, 2001, the United States started its operations to topple the Taliban government in Afghanistan. The other two purposes of the war were to capture Osama Bin Laden and destroy his organization. The operations, while lacking concrete UN coverage, were justified on the basis of self-defense. Despite succeeding in toppling the Taliban government and installing a new government under President Hamid Karzai, the invasion failed to capture Bin Laden or his right arm, Al-Zawahry, although it succeeded in inflicting huge losses on their organization.

The decision to invade Iraq divided not only the American people, but the whole world as well. The decision was arguably unrelated to the September terrorist attacks, but the Bush Administration tried to establish the link between the regime of Saddam Hussein and *Al-Qaeda*. The United States failed to gain UN support, with France, Germany, China, and Russia leading the opposition. The decision also divided the administration, with Secretary of State Colin Powell in clear opposition to it. Later, especially toward the end of his second term in office, President Bush confessed that the invasion was based on weak intelligence information.

This weak intelligence not only influenced the decision, but also its aftermath. The invasion created a new sanctuary for *Al-Qaeda*, who found in occupied Iraq ready targets in American military personnel as well as other Iraqis who were Shiites or even Sunnis. Iran also gained leverage through interference in Iraq, a card it used effectively in negotiations regarding its nuclear program, which arguably started during the reign of the Shah but was secret until news about it started leaking in the early 1990s.

Iraq is a post-World War I creation. Although many of its cities like Baghdad and Basra, had a glorious past during the Muslim Empire, the country itself was a modern creation. Despite modernist trends before the Iraq-Iran war (1980-1989), things changed after the war started given the necessity of imposing control on the widely diverse population and the need to depend on traditional sources of power, which was mainly composed of tribal leaders. The country was also divided on racial and religious lines, with Shiites in the south, Sunnis in the middle, and Kurds in the north. Historical animosities developed over history among these groups, especially given the minority Sunni control since the Ottoman Empire. After the invasion, these divisions gave rise to a civil war that the United States was unable to control. Some news reports, especially in the Middle East, pointed to possible American involvement in the cleansing of the minority Sunni population in cooperation with the Shiite militias.

The continuation of the deteriorating situation in Iraq, and the rise in American casualties, intensified domestic and international opposition. On the Israeli-Palestinian front, the Sharon government intensified its crack down on the second *Intifada* claiming that the United States and Israel were fighting the same enemy. On the other hand, the main European opposition forces, France and Germany, started to reconcile since they needed to join the bandwagon and gain a share in the contracts for rebuilding the country. However, internal divisions were intensifying, and they became a critical issue in the 2004 presidential elections.

The 2004 presidential elections witnessed an important influence of the international dimension in internal American politics, something that was arguably never seen before on such a scale. Saddam Hussein was captured by American troops in late 2003. Some skeptics argued that he was actually caught earlier but news was released only at that time in preparation for the elections. *Al-Qaeda* also had a role to play. Only a few days before the elections, Bin Laden issued a video tape in which he criticized the Bush Administration's policies and threatened the American people. The Bush campaign was already highlighting the security threats the United States was facing and criticizing the rather "soft" approach of the democrats regarding terrorist threats. Bush won a second term in office, leaving the nation even more divided regarding his policies and their repercussions.

On the domestic level, the Bush Administration was racially diverse. Condoleeza Rice was the first black National Security Advisor, and Colin Powell was the first black Secretary of State. However, President Bush also opposed a number of affirmative action initiatives. In 2003, he announced opposition to an affirmative action program at the University of Michigan that targeted minority students and said his administration will challenge it before the Supreme Court.[44] This issue led to early cleavages within the Bush Administration, which only intensified later during the drive to invade Iraq. Secretary of State Colin Powell said he disagreed with the president's position on the Michigan University Case, which had found its way to the Supreme Court. Powell announced his support for the University of Michigan to bolster minority enrollments in its undergraduate and law school programs. On the other hand, Condoleezza Rice said she backed Bush's decision to step into the case before the Supreme Court.[45]

Immigration was another issue that divided the nation during the first Bush Administration, and rose to the forefront even more intensely during his second Administration. In 2004, President Bush announced a program to allow illegal immigrants to legally work in the United States for up to three years in jobs that Americans are "not willing" to do. He argued that the intention of his program was to boost the economy.[46]

The Bush Administration was highly conservative on gay rights issues. The Administration strongly opposed gay marriage, and considered a constitutional amendment to block it.[47] This staunch resistance came at a time when states and the judiciary were taking broad steps on gay rights issues. A clear blow to gay rights opponents came on February 3rd, 2003, when the Massachusetts Supreme Court, in a 4-3 ruling, gave the Massachusetts state Legislature six months to rewrite the state's marriage laws for the benefit of gay couples. The ruling set off a huge controversy not just in the state but also on the national level. A Constitutional amendment became all the more important for the republicans, but without success throughout Bush's two terms in office.[48] Gay marriage became legal in Massachusetts in May 2004.[49] In November 2003, the Supreme Court struck down a Texas State law banning private consensual sex between adults of the same sex by a 6-3 vote.[50] On a closing note, the country's first openly gay bishop was formally consecrated in New Hampshire in November 2003.[51]

Public Opinion Data 1995-2004

African Americans

In 2001, when asked again how well Negros are treated in this country, only 38 percent answered "fairly" or "the same as whites." In the 1960s, 70 and 72 percent had answered "fairly" or "the same as whites."

In response to the question about whether black children have the same chances as white children to get a good education in their community between 80 and 82 percent answered the same chance. The percents are consistent with responses in earlier years.

On the matter of getting affordable housing in their community, 86 and 83 percent answered that blacks had the same chance as whites. These percentages showed an increase over the 1989 and 1991 responses when 71 and 74 percent answered the same chance as whites.

In 2001, black respondents were asked if they believe they received unfair treatment in a variety of situations: shopping, dealing with police, in restaurants, bars and theaters, at work and while using public transit. In none of these contexts did more than 27 percent believe they received unfair treatment.

From 1995 to 1999 on the more general issue of the likelihood that a solution to the problem of black/white relations would ever be worked

Context	Unfairly Treated (%)
Shopping in a store	27
In dealing with police	21
In restaurant, bars, theaters	20
At work	19
While using public transit	5

out, slightly more than 50 percent thought it would always be a problem. In 2001, 45 percent thought it would always be a problem.

And when asked to "rate the state of race relations in the U.S. today," between 43 and 50 percent rated them as "Somewhat or Very Good" from 1998 to 2001.

Jews

In 1998 and 2002, the items included on the national survey Anti-Semitic Index were asked with much the same results as in previous years. Items 9 and 10 (Jews always like to be at the head of things and Jews stick together too much) had the highest support.

In 2003 the public was asked: " Do you think Anti-Semitism, or prejudice against the Jewish people, is currently a very serious problem, somewhat of a problem, not much of a problem, not a problem at all."

The public was divided with 57 percent viewing anti-Semitism as a problem and 39 percent discounting it as a problem. Also in 2003, when asked, "Do you agree or disagree that virtually all positions of influence in the US are open to Jews?" 59 percent agreed and 34 percent disagreed.

Muslim Americans

The first time a question about Muslim Americans appeared on a national survey was in 2004. The item asked whether respondents supported restrictions on Muslim Americans.

Public Support for Restrictions on Muslim Americans

Statement	% Agreed
All Muslim Americans should be required to register their whereabouts with the federal government.	27
Mosques should be closely monitored and surveilled by U.S. law enforcement agencies.	26
U.S. government agencies should profile citizens as potential threats based on being Muslim or having Middle Eastern heritage.	22
Muslim civic and volunteer organizations should be infiltrated by undercover law enforcement agents to keep watch on their activities and fundraising.	29
Agreed with none of the statements.	48
Agreed with at least one of the statements.	44
Agreed with one statement only.	15
Agreed with two of the statements.	11
Agreed with three of the statements.	9
Agreed with all four statements.	9

Source: *Media and Society Research Group*, Cornell University, page 6 (Table 7).

The data show that almost half of the respondents (48 percent) agreed with none of the statements.

When respondents were divided by political party affiliations republicans were more likely to favor placing restrictions on Muslim Americans than were democrats and independents.

Restrictions on Muslim Americans by Party (Percent Agree)

Statement	Rep	Ind	Dem
All Muslim Americans should be required to register their whereabouts.	40	17	24
Mosques should be closely monitored.	34	24	22
U.S. government agencies should profile Muslim citizens.	34	15	17
Muslim civic and volunteer organizations should be infiltrated.	41	27	21

Source: *Media and Society Research Group*, Cornell University, page 6 (Table 8).

As shown below respondents who were more fearful of Muslim Americans favored placing more restrictions on them; as were more religious respondents.

Public Support for Restrictions on Muslim Americans by Level of Fear (Percent Agree)

Statement	Low Fear	High Fear
All Muslim Americans should be required to register their whereabouts.	24	37
Mosques should be closely monitored.	21	42
U.S. government agencies should profile Muslim citizens.	19	31
Muslim civic and volunteer organizations should be infiltrated.	25	42

Source: *Media & Society Research Group*, Cornell University, page 6 (Table 9)

Public Support for Restrictions on Muslim Americans by Personal Religiosity
(Percent Agree)

Statement	Level of Religiosity		
	Low	Moderate	High
All Muslim Americans should be required to register their whereabouts.	15	30	42
Mosques should be closely monitored.	13	33	34
U.S. Government agencies should profile citizens based on being Muslim.	16	24	29
Muslim civic and volunteer organizations should be infiltrated.	19	33	40

We see in the data below that slightly more than half of the male and female respondents had favorable opinions of Muslim Americans. Blacks at 64 percent held more favorable opinions than whites at 53 percent. Younger respondents and those with more years of schooling held more favorable opinions, as did persons with higher incomes.

Respondents held more favorable views of Catholics and Jews than they did of Muslim Americans. Their views of Evangelical Christians were about the same as their views of Muslims. Only Atheists fared worse than Muslim Americans.

A large majority (87 percent) believed Muslim Americans were committed to their religious beliefs. Slightly less than half (47 percent) thought they were respectful of other religions, and only about a third (35 percent) thought they were respectful of women.

When the views of Americans were compared against those of British, French, Italian, Spanish, and German respondents over a range of questions the results showed little difference among countries:

- Muslims are a threat to national security.
- Muslims in your country have become the subject of unjustified criticism and prejudice.
- Muslims have too much, too little, or the right amount of power in your country.

On the first item, British respondents were more likely to see the presence of Muslims as a threat. The Americans, French, and Italians were more likely to see them as the subject of unjustified criticism and the British were most likely to see them as having too much power. Half of the Americans were "not sure."

Opinion of Muslim-Americans

	Favorable %	Unfavorable %	(VOL.) DK/Ref %	(N)**
Total	55	25	20=100	(1000)
Sex				
Male	54	28	18	(477)
Female	55	21	24	(523)
Race				
White	53	25	22	(818)
Non-white	61	22	17	(173)
Black	64	26	10	(109)
Hispanic*	52	26	22	(63)
Race and Sex				
White Men	53	30	17	(391)
White Women	54	20	26	(427)
Age				
Under 30	62	25	13	(158)
30-49	57	22	21	(350)
50-64	54	25	21	(275)
65+	40	30	30	(202)
Sex and Age				
Men under 50	58	27	15	(252)
Women under 50	59	20	21	(256)
Men 50+	47	30	23	(222)
Women 50+	50	24	26	(255)
Education				
College Grad.	65	15	20	(354)
Some College	63	17	20	(236)
High School Grad.	45	33	22	(322)
<H.S. Grad.	41	37	22	(84)
Family Income				
$75,000+	63	21	16	(240)
$50,000-$74,999	54	27	19	(155)
$30,000-$49,999	52	24	24	(205)
$20,000-$29,999	48	23	29	(91)
<$20,000	55	28	17	(150)
Region				
East	60	20	20	(154)

(cont.)

Midwest	53	29	18	(248)
South	54	27	19	(389)
West	53	20	27	(209)
Religious Affiliation				
Total White Protestant	53	26	21	(452)
-Evangelical	53	29	18	(257)
-Non-Evangelical	53	23	24	(195)
White Catholic	61	17	22	(156)
Black Protestant	67	28	5	(71)
Secular	50	22	28	(134)
Party ID				
Republican	48	30	22	(329)
Democrat	61	21	18	(315)
Independent	55	25	20	(282)
Party and Ideology				
Conservative Republican	46	37	17	(213)
Moderate/Liberal Rep.	57	19	24	(106)
Conservative/Mod. Dem.	59	23	18	(207)
Liberal Democrat	70	19	11	(96)

*The designation Hispanic is unrelated to the white-black categorization.

**Sample size applies to "opinion of Muslim-Americans" results. Sample size for "Opinion of Islam" results at least twice the size.

Question: Would you say you have a generally favorable or unfavorable opinion of Islam (…the Muslim religion)?

Is your overall opinion of Muslim Americans very favorable, mostly favorable, mostly unfavorable, or very unfavorable?

Source: Pew Research Center for the People & the Press and Pew Forum on Religion & Public Life. July 2005 Religion and Public Life Survey, Final Topline. July 7-17, 2005. N=2000.

Favorable and Unfavorable Opinions, Muslim Americans Compared with Catholics, Jews, Evangelical Christians, and Atheists

		---Favorable---			----Unfavorable----				
		Total	Very	Mostly	Total	Very	Mostly	(VOL.) Never Heard of	(VOL.) Can't Rate/ Ref
a.F1	Catholics	73	24	49	14	4	10	0	13=100
	Mid-July, 2003	69	21	48	18	6	12	*	13=100
	March, 2002	74	19	55	13	4	9	*	13=100
	Mid-Nov.,2001	78	29	49	8	3	5	*	14=100
	March, 2001	74	19	55	13	3	10	1	12=100
	September, 2000 (RVs)	78	29	49	9	3	6	*	13=100
b.F1	Jews	77	23	54	7	2	5	*	16=100
	Late May, 2005	77	37	40	7	2	5	*	16=100
	Mid-July, 2003	72	20	52	9	3	6	1	18=100
	March, 2002	74	18	56	9	2	7	*	17=100
	Mid-Nov., 2001	75	24	51	7	2	5	*	18=100
	March, 2001	72	16	56	10	2	8	*	18=100
	September, 2000 (RVs)	77	27	50	8	3	5	*	15=100
	June, 1997	82	26	56	9	2	7	1	8=100
c.F1	Evangelical Christians	57	17	40	19	5	14	5	19=100
	Mid-July, 2003	58	18	40	18	6	12	3	21=100
	March, 2002	55	13	42	18	5	13	7	20=100
	March, 2001	55	13	42	16	4	12	8	21=100
	September, 2000 (RVs)	63	21	42	16	3	13	3	18=100
	February, 1996	39	13	26	38	15	23	11	12=100
	July, 1994	43	10	33	32	10	22	11	14=100
	May, 1990	43	12	31	38	19	19	7	12=100
d.F1	Muslim Americans	55	9	46	25	9	16	*	20=100
	Mid-July, 2003	51	10	41	24	9	15	1	24=100
	March, 2002	54	8	46	22	8	14	2	22=100
	Mid-Nov., 2001	59	15	44	17	5	12	1	23=100
	March, 2001	45	7	38	24	8	16	4	27=100
	September, 2000 (RVs)	50	11	39	21	8	13	2	27=100
e.F1	Atheists, that is, people who don't believe in God	35	7	28	50	28	22	0	15=100
	Mid-July 2003	34	7	27	52	33	19	*	14=100
	March, 2002	34	5	29	54	31	23	*	12=100
	Mid-November 2001	32	7	25	49	28	21	*	19=100

Source: Pew Research Center for the People & the Press and Pew Forum on Religion & Public Life.

The Americans, Germans, and British were most likely to object if their child wanted to marry a Muslim.

And only a majority of the French respondents, at 69 percent, said they had friends who were Muslims.

Gays and Lesbians

From November 1996 through July 2003 between 44 and 60 percent of the respondents thought that homosexual relations between consenting adults should be legal and between 42 percent and 54 percent thought it should be considered an acceptable alternative life style.

Between 83 and 89 percent believed homosexuals should have equal rights in terms of job opportunities.

On the matter of whether homosexuality is something a person is born with or a function of upbringing and environment or both between 55 and 48 percent said they thought it was a function of upbringing and environment or both.

Sixty-two and 68 percent supported gay marriages in 1996 and 1999, but only 45 percent opposed a Constitutional amendment that would bar gay marriages. And between 46 and 57 percent opposed a law that would allow homosexual couples to legally form civil unions.

The following item appeared for the first time on a national survey in March 1996: "Do you think marriages between same-sex couples should or should not be recognized by the law as valid, with the same rights as traditional marriages?"

In 1996, 68 percent said such marriages should not be valid and in 1999, 62 percent said they should not be valid.

Going back to questions asked in earlier decades, we find that between 44 and 60 percent of respondents believe homosexual relations between consenting adults should be legal when asked on polls in 1996, 1999, 2001, 2002, 2003, and 2004. And between 42 and 54 percent said they believe homosexuality should be considered an acceptable alternative life style when included on national polls in 1996, 1997, 1999, 2001, 2002, 2003, and 2004.

Between 83 and 89 percent thought homosexuals should have equal rights in terms of job opportunities from 1996 through 2004.

A significant increase in the percentage of respondents who believe homosexuality is something a person is born with occurred in the decade from 1995 to 2004 compared to the previous decade. Between 1995 and 2004 between 31 and 40 percent believe homosexuality is something a person is born with compared to less than 20 percent between 1982 and 1989.

"Would you favor or oppose a law that would allow homosexual couples to legally form civil unions, giving them some of the legal rights of married couples?" was asked for the first time in October 2000, and between 48 and 57 percent said they opposed such a law.

And when asked for the first time in 2003 whether respondents favored or opposed a constitutional amendment that would define marriage as between a man and a woman thus barring marriages between gay and lesbian couples, between 47 and 53 percent favored such an amendment and between 44 and 47 percent opposed such an amendment.

When asked for the first time in 2001: "Would you like a see homosexuality be more widely accepted in this nation, less widely accepted, or is the acceptance of homosexuality about right?" between 28 and 30 percent answered "more widely accepted," between 31 and 35 percent said "less widely accepted" and between 31 and 34 percent said it was "about right."

Concerning service in the military, the following question was asked for the first time in January 2000.

"As you may know, under the current military policy, no one in the military is asked whether or not they are gay. But if they reveal that they are gay or they engage in homosexual activity, they will be discharged from the military. Do you personally think gays should be allowed to serve openly in the military, gays should be allowed to serve under the current policy, or gays should not be allowed to serve in the military under any circumstances?"

The responses were divided such that 41 percent answered "serve openly," 38 percent answered "serve under current policy," and 17 percent responded "not serve under any circumstances."

Immigration

During this decade, the levels of immigration item showed a change such that from 2000 through 2004 between 13 and 17 percent favored an increase in immigration. Those percentages represent the highest levels supporting an increase since the question was first included on national polls in 1946.

When asked in 2001, 2002, and 2003, about whether "On the whole immigration is a good thing or a bad thing for the country today" between 52 and 62 percent said it was a "good thing" and only between 4 and 5 percent said it was "mixed."

During the same period when asked "How satisfied are you with the treatment of immigrants in the United States?" a majority of the respondents, between 54 and 58 percent, answered "satisfied."

Abortion

Between May 2000 and March 2003, the items first asked in 1993 about whether abortion should be generally available appeared on national polls with the following results:

	Generally Available (%)	Available But With Stricter Limits (%)	Not Permitted (%)
May 2000	37	39	22
March 2001	33	43	23
March 2003	39	38	28

We see little change in opinions even going back to 1993 when the distribution was:

	Percent
Generally Available	42
Available But With Stricter Limits	36
Not Permitted	24

Less than a quarter of the respondents advocated that abortions not be permitted.

In February 2004, slightly more than a third (36 percent) favored making it more difficult for a woman to get an abortion.

Affirmative Action

The year 1995 was the first time a question about affirmative action appeared on a national poll and 58 percent of the respondents answered that they favored affirmative action programs.

In 2002, the public was asked: "In order to overcome past discrimination, do you favor or oppose affirmative action programs?" Sixty-three percent answered that they favored such programs and 29 percent said they opposed them.

They were then asked, "Do you favor or oppose affirmative action programs which give special preferences to qualified blacks, women and other minorities in hiring and education?" to which 57 percent answered "favor" and 35 percent answered "oppose."

And, "All in all, do you think affirmative action programs designed to increase the number of black and minority students on college campuses are a good thing, are fair or unfair?" Sixty percent thought they were a good thing, 30 percent a bad thing, 47 percent fair, and 42 percent unfair.

"We should make every possible effort to improve the position of blacks and other minorities even if it means giving them preferential treatment," 72 percent disagreed, and 24 percent agreed.

In a 2003 national survey, 60 percent of the respondents said that "affirmative action programs are good," and 30 percent said they are "bad." Only 47 percent said they were "fair." Forty-two percent said they were "unfair." Women were more likely than men to think they were good (65 v. 54 percent) and fair (52 v. 43 percent). And blacks and Hispanics were more likely than whites to think they were good and fair.

	Good (%)	Fair (%)
White	54	45
Black	87	58
Hispanic	77	70

In 2003, the public was again asked whether they support programs that help blacks, women, and other minorities get jobs and education, to which 66 percent of white women and 48 percent of white men said they favored such programs.

Then when asked whether they support programs that raise the number of minority college students, again 60 percent of white women and 48 percent of white men said they thought it was a good thing.

Between 1995 and 2003 the public was asked, "In general, do you think we need to increase, keep the same, or decrease affirmative action programs in this country?" Between 6 and 11 percent of blacks did not favor a reduction in affirmative action programs and between 26 and 41 percent of whites did support a decrease in affirmative action programs.

When opinions about affirmative action programs were divided by party ideology, the results looked like this:

	Good (%)	Fair (%)
Conservative Republicans	36	26
Moderate Republicans	57	47
Conservative/Moderate Democrats	61	55
Liberal Democrats	71	66

On the matter of who has been affected by affirmative action, in the 2003 survey, 15 percent said they had been directly affected by affirmative action: 11 percent reported being hurt and 4 percent reported being helped. Among blacks 14 percent said they had been helped and 5 percent hurt. Only 2 percent of whites said they had been helped and 13 percent reported that they were hurt. Four percent of Hispanics said they were helped and 4 percent said they were hurt.

Between 1995 and 2003 respondents who favored affirmative action programs increased from 46 to 57 percent.

In 2003, when respondents were asked: "If two equally qualified students, one white and one black applied to a major US college or university, who do you think would have the better chance of being accepted to the college?" 36 percent said each would have the same chance, 31 percent said the white student and 29 percent said the black student. Among the white respondents 34 percent said the black student and 24 percent said the white student; 38 percent said the same chance. Among the black respondents, 67 percent said the white student, 5 percent said the black student and 24 percent said the same chance.

When respondents were asked in 2003 whether they had been directly affected by affirmative action, 14 percent of the black respondents reported having been helped and 5 percent reported having been hurt. Among the white respondents, 2 percent reported having been helped, and 13 percent reported that they were hurt. Among Hispanics, 4 percent said they were helped and 4 percent said they were hurt.

Notes

1. Beth Kampschror. 2004. NATO hands over Bosnia peacekeeping to EU. *USA Today*. December 2. Available through:
    http://www.usatoday.com/news/world/2004-12-02-eu-bosnia_x.htm?csp=36. Access Date: November 24, 2008.
2. Mike Hanna. 1995. "Peace clock" is ticking in Bosnia. CNN. Available through:
    http://www.cnn.com/WORLD/Bosnia/updates/dec95/12-15/sarajevo/index.html. Access Date: November 24, 2008.
3. Diana Johnstone. 1999. Kosovo and Yugoslavia bombing: The war NATO wanted. Available through:
    http://www.afn.org/~iguana/archives/1999_05/19990509.html. Access Date: November 24, 2008.
4. Desert Dispatch. Kosovo: An independent headache for U.S. Available Through:
    http://www.desertdispatch.com/opinion/kosovo_2616___article.html/independence_united.html. Access Date: November 24, 2008.
5. U.S. Department of State. Remarks with Kosovo President Fatmir Sejdiu and Kosovo Prime Minister Hashim Thaci. Available through:
    http://www.state.gov/secretary/rm/2008/07/107225.htm. Access Date: November 24, 2008.

6.   Ted Galen Carpenter. 1992. Setting a Dangerous Precedent in Somalia. Cato Foreign Policy Briefing No. 20. December 18. Available through: *http://cato.org/pubs/fpbriefs/fpb-020.html*. Access Date: November 24, 2008.

7.   Global Policy Forum. Available through: *http://www.globalpolicy.org/security/issues/somalindex.htm*. Access Date: November 24, 2008.

8.   Nation Master. Available through: *http://www.nationmaster.com/encyclopedia/Mogadiscio*. Access Date: November 24, 2008.

9.   Wikipedia: The Free Encyclopedia. Available through: *http://en.wikipedia.org/wiki/Battle_of_Mogadishu_(1993)#Policy_changes*. Access Date: November 24, 2008.

10. United States Government Accountability Office. 2008. Somalia: Several Challenges Limit U.S. and International Stabilization, Humanitarian, and Development Efforts. Available through: *http://www.gao.gov/new.items/d08351.pdf*. Access Date: November 24, 2008.

11. Pirates of the Arabian. Foreign Affairs. Available through: *http://www.foreignaffairs.org/background/default#botn2008-10-08*. Access Date: November 28, 2008.

12. Al-Ahram. November 28, 2008. Available through: *http://www.ahram.org.eg/Index.asp?CurFN=fron2.htm&DID=9781*. Access Date: November 28, 2008.

13. The White House. Progress for Gay and Lesbian Americans: The Clinton-Gore Administration-A Record of Progress. Available through: *http://clinton4.nara.gov/WH/Accomplishments/ac399.html*. Access Date: November 28, 2008.

14. American Patriot Friends Network. Gay Martyr Used to Promote Hate Crime Legislation. Available through: *http://www.apfn.org/THEWINDS/1998/10/gay_martyr.html*. Access Date: November 28, 2008.

15. Center for Military Readiness. Gay Language School Students Dismissed. Available through: *http://www.cmrlink.org/HMilitary.asp?docID=170*. Access Date: November 29, 2008.

16. David Burelli and Charles Dale. 2005. Homosexuals and U.S. Military Policy: Current Issues. CBS Report for Congress. Updated May 27. Available through: *http://www.fas.org/sgp/crs/natsec/RL30113.pdf*. Access Date: November 29, 2008.

17. Wikipedia: The Free Encyclopedia. Available through: *http://en.wikipedia.org/wiki/Barry_Winchell*. Access Date: November 29, 2008.

18. Norma M. Riccucci, Marcia K. Meyers, Irene Lurie, and Jun Seop Han. 2004. The Implementation of Welfare Reform Policy: The Role of Public Managers in Front-Line Practices. *Public Administration Review* 64(4): 438-448.

19. Clinton Signs Welfare Reform Bill, Angers Liberals. Available through: *http://www-cgi.cnn.com/ALLPOLITICS/1996/news/9608/22/welfare.sign/*. Access Date: November 29, 2008.

20. Dan Froomkin. Welfare's Changing Face. Washington Post.com. Available through: *http://www.washingtonpost.com/wp-srv/politics/special/welfare/welfare.htm*. Access Date: November 29, 2008.

21. This topic has been discussed extensively especially in Public Administration and Constitutional Law literature. See for example:

- Jody Freeman. 2003. Extending Public Law Norms Through Privatization. *Harvard Law Review* 116(5): 1285-1352, and
- David Rosenbloom and Suzanne Piotrowski. 2005. Outsourcing Constitutional and Administrative Law Norms. *Public Administration Review* 35 (2): 103-121.

22. Katherine N. Naff. To Look Like America. In Julian Dolan and David H. Rosenbloom (eds). *Representative Bureaucracy: Classic Readings and Continuing Controversies*. New York: M.E. Sharpe.

23. Famous American Trials. Available through: *http://www.law.umkc.edu/faculty/projects/ftrials/Simpson/simpson.htm*. Access Date: December 4, 2008.

24. Deborah Barnes. Research in the News: Creating a Cloned Sheep Named Dolly. *National Institute of Health*. Available through: *http://science-education.nih.gov/home2.nsf/Educational+ResourcesTopicsGenetics/BC5086E34E4DBA0085256CCD006F01CB*. Access Date: December 2, 2008.

25. Kyla Dunn. 2005. The Politics of Stem Cells. PBS. Available through: *http://www.pbs.org/wgbh/nova/sciencenow/dispatches/050413.html*. Access Date: December 2, 2008.

26. CNN. 1998. Clinton: Iraq has abused its last chance. December 16. Available through: *http://www.cnn.com/US/9812/16/clinton.iraq.speech/*. Access Date. December 1, 2008.

27. *Time*. 2001. Twin Perils of Love and War. June 24. Available through: *http://www.time.com/time/magazine/article/0,9171,138658,00.html?iid=chixsphere*. Access Date: December 1, 2008.

28. David L. Harten. 2001. Clinton's Worst Crimes. The Ornery American. January 26. Available through: *http://www.ornery.org/essays/2001-01-26-1.html*. Access Date: December 1, 2008.

29. United Nations Special Commission. Available through: *http://www.un.org/Depts/unscom/unscom.htm#MANDATE*. Access Date: December 1, 2008.

30. Xinhau News Agency. 2003. UN Security Council resolutions on Iraq since 1990. Available through: *http://news.xinhuanet.com/english/2003-05/22/content_881820.htm*. Access Date: December 1, 2008.

31. BBC News. 1998. World: Middle East Unscom withdraws monitors from Iraq. November 11. Available through: *http://news.bbc.co.uk/2/hi/middle_east/212123.stm*. Access Date: December 1, 2008.

32. Global Policy Forum. Oil-for-Food Programme. Available through: *http://www.globalpolicy.org/security/sanction/iraq1/oilindex.htm*. Access Date: December 2, 2008.

33. Sharon Otterman. 2005. Iraq: Oil for Food Scandal. *Council on Foreign Relations*. October 28. Available through: *http://www.cfr.org/publication/7631/iraq.html*. Access Date: December 2, 2008.

34. Global Security.org. Khobar Towers. Available through: *http://www.globalsecurity.org/military/facility/khobar.htm*. Access Date: December 3, 2008.

35. Global Security.org. Attacks on US Embassies in Kenya and Tanzania. Available through:

http://www.globalsecurity.org/security/ops/98emb.htm. Access Date: December 2, 2008.

36. CNN. 1998. U.S. missiles pound targets in Afghanistan, Sudan. August 21. Available through: *http://www.cnn.com/US/9808/20/us.strikes.02/.* Access Date: December 2, 2008.

37. Guy Gugliotta and Juliet Eilperin. 1998. Tough Response Appeals to Clinton's Critics. *Washington Post.* Available through: *http://www.washingtonpost.com/wp-srv/politics/special/clinton/stories/react082198.htm.* Access Date: December 2, 2008.

38. Raphael Perl and Ronald O'Rourke. Terrorist Attack on USS Cole: Background and Issues for Congress. CRS Report for Congress. Available through: *http://fl1.findlaw.com/news.findlaw.com/cnn/docs/crs/coleterrattck13001.pdf.* Access Date: December 3, 2008.

39. CNN. 2000. U.S. official sees similarities between USS Cole blast and embassy attacks. October 23. Available through: *http://archives.cnn.com/2000/US/10/23/uss.cole.01/.* Access Date: December 3, 2008.

40. BBC. 2000: "Provocative" mosque visits sparks riots. Available through: *http://news.bbc.co.uk/onthisday/hi/dates/stories/september/28/newsid_3687000/3687762.stm.* Access Date: December 5, 2008.

41. MSN Encarta. Disputed Presidential Election of 2000. Available through: *http://encarta.msn.com/encyclopedia_681500368/Disputed_Presidential_Election_of_2000.html.* Access Date: December 5, 2008.

42. *Op cit.*

43. Al Gore's concession speech is available on Youtube through: *http://www.youtube.com/swf/l.swf?swf=http%3A//s.ytimg.com/yt/swf/cps-vfl67854. swf&video_id=GyKlcQ_HiD4&rel=1&showsearch=1&eurl=http%3A//video. search.yahoo.com/video/play%3Fp%3D2000%2Bpresidential%2Belections% 26ei%3DUTF-8%26fr%3Dyfp-t-120%26tnr%3D21%26vid%&iurl=http%3A// i4.ytimg.com/vi/GyKlcQ_HiD4/hqdefault.jpg&sk=NYDckKe2UKMkjQsqSGeQF2 yljRR7Yy4MC&use_get_video_info=1&load_modules=1.* Access Date: December 5, 2008.

44. CNN. 2003. Bush criticizes university "quota system": Debate on affirmative action heats up. January 16. Available through: *http://www.cnn.com/2003/ALLPOLITICS/01/15/bush.affirmativeaction/.* Access Date: December 6, 2008.

45. *USA Today.* 2003. Powell disagrees with Bush on affirmative action case. Available through: *http://www.usatoday.com/news/washington/2003-01-19-powell_x.htm.* Access Date: December 6, 2008.

46. CNN. 2004. Bush pushes for immigrant worker plan. Available through: *http://www.cnn.com/2004/ALLPOLITICS/01/10/bush.radio/index.html.* Access Date: December 6, 2008.

47. CNN. 2003. Bush wants marriage reserved for heterosexuals: "we ought to codify that." Available through: *http://www.cnn.com/2003/ALLPOLITICS/07/30/bush.gay.marriage/.* Access Date: December 5, 2008.

48. CNN. 2004. Massachusetts court rules ban on gay marriage unconstitutional. Available through: *http://www.cnn.com/2003/LAW/11/18/samesex.marriage.ruling/index.html.* Access Date: December 5, 2008.

49. *USA Today*. 2008. Mass. Gov. signs gay marriage bill. Available through: *http://www.usatoday.com/news/nation/2008-07-31-marriage_N.htm*. Access Date: December 5, 2008.
50. CNN. 2003. Supreme Court strokes down Texas sodomy law : Ruling establishes new legal ground in privacy, experts say. Available through: *http://www.cnn.com/2003/LAW/06/26/scotus.sodomy/*. Access Date: December 5, 2008.
51. BBC News. 2003. Massachusetts backs gay marriage. November 18. Available through: *http://news.bbc.co.uk/2/hi/americas/3281017.stm*. Access Date: December 5, 2008.

14

The United States between 2005 and 2008: A New Social Movement on the Rise

The second term of President Bush in office witnessed a number of social stresses and disaffection. The deterioration of the situation in Iraq became ever clearer, and critics argued that there was never a plan for the post-occupation phase. American casualties increased, the internal situation in the country deteriorated into civil war, and the promises of President Bush to spread democracy in the Middle East were dashed when the Administration retreated from its support after seeing the rise of Islamists through democratic elections, especially in Egypt and the Palestinian territories. More importantly, the hypocrisy of the Bush administration regarding its position on democracy became a topic of international criticism given the fact that it had to cooperate with the autocratic governments in the region in order to counter the Iranian nuclear ambition, control the strife in Iraq, and contain the Hamas government in the Palestinian territories. In short, when democracy was weighed against traditional security considerations, democracy clearly lost.

The promises of the Bush Administration gave some hope that autocratic rulers in the region would be pressured to open up their political systems. Reforms did take place in some countries but as later events showed, these were more of bending to the storm than being real and long-term reforms. For example, Egypt established a National Council for Human Rights in 2003, and President Mubarak proposed a constitutional amendment to allow direct popular presidential elections to replace the referendum system, which has been the mechanism to choose the president since the revolution of 1952. But the reforms were clearly tactical given the rejection of limiting the president's terms in office to two terms. The later wording of Article 76 (which speaks about the selection of the president) led to widespread disappointment given the restrictions it imposed on who has the right to run for president.

The referendum on the Constitutional amendment witnessed serious violations by the security apparatus, and the 2005 parliamentary elections, in which the Muslim Brothers won 20 percent of the seats in the Parliament, witnessed serious violations especially toward its later stages. Ayman Nour, who came in second after President Mubarak in the presidential race, lost his seat in these Parliamentary elections and was sentenced to five years in prison based on charges that were believed to be forged by the Egyptian authorities. The denouncements and criticisms of the United States did not lead to the release of Nour, who was sentenced in December 2005, shortly after the end of the Egyptian Parliamentary elections. He was only released after President Obama came to office and shortly before his visit to Egypt to address the Muslim world in June 2009.

Other developments were taking place on the Israeli-Palestinian front. Israel's Prime Minister Ariel Sharon announced the "Disengagement Plan" in December 2003 to withdraw from Gaza and dismantle Israeli settlements there.[1] Israel completed its withdrawal in September 2005 after almost thirty-eight years of occupying the narrow coastal area since June 5, 1967.[2] President Bush had endorsed the Israeli plan, calling Sharon's actions "historic and courageous."[3]

The most alarming threat from the region from the Administration's perspective was the winning of a sweeping majority by Hamas in the Palestinian Parliamentary elections in 2005/2006. Hamas was classified as a terrorist organization by Israel, the United States, and the European Union. The international community, led by the United States, and in cooperation with regional powers, especially Saudi Arabia and Egypt, worked on isolating the Hamas government. International sanctions led to severely reducing available health care, education, and other basic services and dramatically increased unemployment and malnutrition. In the midst of these conditions, fighting erupted between Hamas and Fatah factions in 2007, leading to widespread criticisms among the Palestinian and Arab populations since this fighting led to fostering claims that the Palestinians were not worthy of an independent state. The Gaza blockade, which followed Hamas control of the strip after infighting with Fatah troops, led to a serious humanitarian crisis that claimed the lives of many civilians.[4]

The most impressive development was the decision of Libyan President Muammar Qaddafi to make Libya completely free of internationally banned weapons. President George W. Bush and Prime Minister Tony Blair hailed the Libyan decision. Libya continued steps toward reconciliation and solving long-standing deadlocks with Western countries. The Bush Administration was quick to attribute this development to its efforts to spread democracy and freedom in the world.

Despite these rather limited successes in achieving some degree of democratic opening in the Middle East, reflected in the decisions by some regional rulers to hold elections, establish guarantees for human rights, or denounce support for international terrorism, the American image in the world was critically defamed and its credibility strongly questioned when photographs of abuse in the Abu Ghraib prison in Iraq were aired between October and December 2003. This scandal, and the weak response to it by the Administration, raised even more questions about the cause of the war on Iraq, supposedly to free the Iraqi people from the torturous and brutal regime of Saddam Hussein.[5] These criticisms escalated during Bush's second term in office, making him even worse than the "lame duck" metaphor of a president in his second term.

The graphic displays of the abuses in the Iraqi prison, originally established during the rule of Saddam Hussein, revealed an image of a Presidential Administration that was willing to compromise the values on which the American society was built for some ideological or business interests that proved fatal. While Neoconservatism came to the forefront when Bush was first elected as president in 2001, raising concerns especially across the Atlantic, its downfall took less than half a decade. And when President Bush started his second term, many of the important neocon figures, such as Rumsfeld and Wolfowitz, were already losing confidence even among their peers.

The abuse of prisoners in Abu Ghraib, preceded by evidence of similar abuses in Guantanamo Bay prison, set off a heated debate about the Administration's moral standards, which revealed clear ethical problems and moral ambiguity. The abuses also revealed the inability of the Administration to deal with the situation in Iraq. As the war in Iraq took an unexpected turn through the rise of insurgency and *Al-Qaeda* operations, the infiltration of security and intelligence services from other regional powers especially Iran, Syria, and Israel, and the de facto division of the country into separate power zones, thousands of innocent Iraqis were sent to Abu Ghraib in addition to insurgents and common criminals. The reaction of the Administration toward the use of torture disappointed a wide segment of the population as well as international public opinion. The Administration basically blamed the torturous practices on "a few bad eggs." Little effort was done to hold those at the top of the command hierarchy responsible, although the reservists who had engaged in the abuse insisted that they were responsive to orders from higher ups to "soften up" the detainees for interrogation.[6]

As usual in American politics, the Supreme Court of the United States interfered to restore balance to the system, which became heavily executive-dominated, and to protect Constitutional values. The Court ruled in a number of cases in support of constitutional and international law rights for detainees in Guantanamo, mainly their right to a free and fair trial. In 2004, in *Hamdi et al. v. Rumsfeld*, the Court ruled that although Congress authorized the detention of combatants in certain circumstances, due process demands that a citizen held in the United States as an enemy combatant be given a meaningful opportunity to contest the factual basis for that detention before a neutral decision maker.[7] This ruling narrowly held for citizen detainees.

In a landmark decision on June 28, 2004, the Court ruled in *Rasul et al. v. Bush* that foreign nationals imprisoned without charge at the Guantanamo Bay interrogation camps were entitled to bring legal action challenging their captivity in American federal civilian courts. The petitioners were two Australians and twelve Kuwaitis captured during the hostilities in Afghanistan and held in military custody in Guantanamo Bay Naval Base. The petitioners argued that they had never been combatants against the United States or engaged in terrorist acts, and that they have never been charged with wrongdoing, permitted to consult counsel, or provided access to courts of other tribunals.[8]

Another major rebuke by the Supreme Court to the Bush Administration came in June 2006, when the Court ruled by a 5 to 3 vote that the president had overstepped his power in ordering war criminal trials for Guantanamo detainees without specific authority from Congress. These tribunals started in the aftermath of the 9/11 attacks. The first prisoner to face war crime charges before these tribunals was Salim Ahmed Hamdan, Bin Laden's private driver who was captured in Afghanistan in 2001 and taken to the Guantanamo prison. When the officer jurors were selected and the trial began, Hamdan was excluded from the courtroom. His lawyers appealed this exclusion all the way to the Supreme Court, arguing that the executive branch was making rules as well as enforcing them. The court said that the procedures set up by the president violate both the Uniform Code of Military Justice and the laws of war set out in the Geneva Conventions. The ruling stipulated that nothing in the court's precedents, or in the post-September 11 actions of Congress, is a sweeping authorization for the president to establish special military commissions whenever he deems necessary.[9]

Another stunning defeat for the Bush Administration's policy regarding "enemy combatants" followed on June 12, 2008, in *Boumediene et al. v. Bush*. In a 5 to 4 decision, the Court ruled that detainees held at Guantanamo Bay have a constitutional right to challenge their detentions in Federal court and that congressional legislation has failed to provide a reasonable substitute for such a hearing. The ruling invalidated portions of the 2005 Detainees Treatment Act, which provided that "no court, justice, or judge shall have jurisdiction to ... consider ... an application for ... habeas corpus filed by or on behalf of an alien detained ... at Guantanamo" and the 2006 Military Commissions Act, which denies judicial jurisdiction "relating to any aspect of detention, transfer, treatment, trial, or conditions of confinement" of a detained alien determined to be an enemy combatant.[10]

Despite American policies and international cooperation against terrorism, *Al-Qaeda* was able to deliver a painful strike against Great Britain, the main ally of the United States in the war on Iraq, on July 7, 2005. The London bombings raised widespread international criticism given that they were directed against innocent civilians who were taking the subway to their work in the morning. This operation and others similar to it encouraged policies such as kidnapping suspected terrorists and sending them to countries that practice torture, and giving a broad authority to the intelligence community to spy on private communication. This time, however, the brutality of the London attacks did not reduce opposition to policies that violate the spirit as well as the explicit words of the American Constitution.

The brutality of the attacks and the graphic pictures of the victims also raised widespread criticism in the Muslim world, even amongst fundamentalist groups such as *Islamic Jihad*. The gulf started to widen between *Jihad* members in Egyptian and other Arab prisons on the one hand, and those members living abroad, led by Ayman Al-Zawahry, on the other. Many of the *Jihad* leaders became highly critical of the indiscriminate killings employed by *Al-Qaeda* leaders. Sayyid Imam, the founder and *Mufti* (religious scholar) of *Al-Jihad* organization wrote a series of theoretical revisions that criticized the ideology of Ayman Al-Zawahry and Osama Bin Laden. He mainly criticized their criminal activities against civilians and their betrayal of America by obtaining entry visas (considered in the view of Imam as a contract of peaceful entry that any Muslim should respect) and then violating the conditions of these visas. Imam also focused his criticism on the results of what he perceived as adventurous and uncalculated acts of Al-Zawahry and Bin Laden, which led to the destruction of the Islamic state in Afghanistan and the catastrophe in Iraq.[11]

On the domestic level, hurricane Katrina hit the country hard and awakened feelings of discrimination and exclusion within the American society. On August 28, 2005, Katrina arrived at the Gulf of Mexico. By the time it ended, it caused the most destruction in terms of economic costs that any hurricane had ever caused.[12] With the massive destruction and loss of lives in Louisiana, Katrina exposed the failure of the government at all levels and its inability to cope with disaster management in the post-9/11 era. The Congressional report on the government's reaction accused the Bush Administration of disregarding ample warnings of the threat to New Orleans and of failing to execute emergency plans or share information that would have saved lives. The resignation of the Federal Emergency Management Agency director Michael Brown did not satisfy public contempt and accusations of the government.[13] Accusations of discrimination against blacks mounted during and in the aftermath of the hurricane. Katrina was another occasion when Americans and people all over the world wondered how the Bush Administration could provide such huge resources to promoting democracy abroad while racial discrimination and poverty at home were paramount.

Interestingly, Bush had used the race card in addressing his plan to privatize social security. While no sweeping changes took place in the system throughout Bush's presidency, his Administration paid special attention to the topic given the problems the system was facing, especially with the near retirement of early baby boomers, and the fact that Social Security was one of the hotly debated issues in the presidential race of 2004. In 2005, Bush suggested that opposition to his privatization plan was based on the notion that some minorities cannot be trusted with their own money.[14] President Bush even used references to race in dismissing opposition to his policies in Afghanistan and Iraq. In a press conference in November 2004, shortly after winning a second term in office, President Bush said, "I simply do not agree with those who either say overtly or believe that certain societies cannot be free. It's just not a part of my thinking."[15]

Toward the end of Bush's presidency, the United States and the international economy at large faced a serious crisis, which also clearly had an effect on the result of the presidential elections in 2008. The economic crisis affected millions of Americans, with businesses closing and thousands of employees losing their jobs. Explanations of the crisis revolved around the issue of credit—a central pillar of the American economy and society, and actually a main reason for its continued growth until new lines of credit dried up and available sources to finance business became in short supply. The causes of this situation were mainly attributed to bad mortgages and a housing bubble, resulting from overextension of lending to unqualified borrowers. Massive losses caused banks to tighten their lending requirements, and others had just failed. While the Bush Administration started a bail out plan to help alleviate the stresses on important sectors, the prospects of a quick recovery appeared dim as 2008 was drawing to a close.

This crisis revealed the vulnerability of the capitalist economy and the dangers it might cause to the society at large. Amidst these conditions, coupled with a thirst for ending international engagements, which were apparently leading nowhere, the 2008 presidential race was heating up. The Republican Party primaries concluded relatively early with Vietnam War veteran and long-term politician John McCain winning the party's nomination. The Democratic Party primaries were exceptionally long and intense. Former first lady Hillary Clinton witnessed an unexpected and serious challenge from the young black candidate, Senator Barack Obama. With his charismatic leadership and consistency of positions, especially regarding his objection to the war in Iraq, Obama was able to win the Democratic nomination after a long and exhausting race.

Obama's campaign was a clear success story. Not only was he able to bring together a broad segment of the American society, especially middle-class Americans, in support for social change, tax, health, and social security reform, and for regaining the credibility of the American system internationally, his main success was to give motivation to a whole young generation of college students who were participating in the elections for the first time in their lives. This generation appeared to be clearly more liberal, less tied to traditional ideological cleavages, and sincerely aspiring to dramatic change. Obama was able to address this segment and mobilize their efforts. Their contributions ranged from a few dollars and volunteer efforts in the campaign, to such rather funny appearances as those of "the Obama Girl."

The election of Barack Obama as president ushered in a new phase in American history. With African and Muslim origins, this event signaled that the American society has passed through a long history of development. It also signaled to the rest of the world that Americans are always ready to change. Colin Powell's support of Obama for president and his contention that even being Muslim should not be an obstacle against any American child's dream to become president gained attention in the Arab and Muslim world, and raised expectations about new and better years ahead.

The higher expectations facing Obama in his first years in office might be counterproductive though. The new president is facing mounting economic and social problems, in addition to two unresolved wars and continuous terrorist threats. Shortly after Obama's elections, Ayman Al-Zawahry released a new video tape in which he criticized Obama as being a fake Muslim and compared him to Malcolm X, whom he considered a true Muslim and great leader. This tape was interpreted as a result of the shock these terrorists had received and the resulting weakened credibility to see a man from African and Muslim origins being elected to the highest office in the United States.

The choice of Rahm Emanuel, who has deep Zionist roots, as White House Chief of Staff raised suspicions in the Arab world and was welcomed in Israel. The new president's choice of Hillary Clinton as Secretary of State, and his decision to keep Gates as Secretary of Defense, reflected his campaign promise to bring Americans together to face the challenges ahead. But these challenges are daunting, and will need tough decisions that will eventually shape the orientations of the young generation that helped bring Obama to power. The president's decisions and policies to address the country's domestic and international problems will create the environment for the political upbringing of today's teenagers and young people who helped elect Obama. A good number of this cohort will be starting their careers by the time Obama's first term in office comes to an end, and their judgment of his performance will be an important consideration in judging the state of the American society at the beginning of the second decade of the twenty-first century.

Public Opinion Data 2005-2008

African Americans

Looking now at the current time, we see the results of the following three items that appeared on national polls in 2007.

Which of these statements comes closer to your views: Racial discrimination is the main reason why many black people can't get ahead OR blacks who can't get ahead are mostly responsible for their own condition.

	All adults (%)	Whites (%)	Blacks (%)	Hispanics (%)
Racial Discrimination	19	15	30	24
Blacks responsible for their own condition	66	71	53	59
Neither/Both (VOL)	9	8	14	8
Don't Know/Refused	6	6	3	9
	100	100	100	100
Number of Respondents	3086	1536	1007	388

Note: Whites include only non-Hispanic whites. Blacks include only non-Hispanic blacks.
Hispanics are of any race. Pew Research Center.

A majority of whites, blacks, and Hispanics agreed that blacks are responsible for their own condition.

On the matter of affirmative action programs twice as many black respondents (78 percent) as white respondents (39 percent) favored them.

And finally when asked in 2007 "What about the future of blacks? Will life be better, the same, or worse?" Fifty-six percent of white respondents thought it would be better compared to 44 percent of blacks. Only 6 percent of white respondents thought it would be worse compared to 21 percent of black respondents. Slightly less than a third of white and black respondents thought it would be about the same.

Jews

In items included in a 2007 national survey, 31 percent of Americans believe Jews are more loyal to Israel than to the U.S.

When asked in 2005 and 2007:

"Do you believe Jews were responsible for the death of Christ?"
30 and 27 percent answered "yes."

Fifteen percent said they believe Jews have too much power in the U.S. and 19 and 20 percent thought they had too much power in the business world in 2005 and 2007.

The 2007 survey also found that 55 percent believe that Jews have special commitments to social justice and civil rights.

Sixty-five percent agree that Jews contribute much to the cultural life of America and 79 percent see as positive Jewish emphasis on the importance of family life.

Muslim Americans

In 2005, when respondents were asked their impression of Muslim Americans, 55 percent answered "favorable," 25 percent answered "unfavorable" and 20 percent had no opinion. Blacks, persons under 30 years of age, college graduates, respondents with annual incomes of more than $75,000, and liberal democrats held the most favorable views.

In 2006, 49 percent of the respondents believed that Muslims living in the United States were loyal to the United States. Fifty percent did not believe Muslim Americans were sympathetic to the al-Queda terrorist organization, 34 percent thought they were sympathetic.

On other issues 87 percent said that they thought Muslim Americans were committed to their religious beliefs, 44 percent thought that they were "too extreme" in their religious beliefs, 47 percent that they "were not respectful" of other religions and 35 percent believed that they were "not respectful of women."

Fifty-nine percent would not be in favor of requiring Muslim Americans to carry a special ID card or to undergo more intensive security checks at airports. And 59 percent responded "no" when asked if they had feelings of prejudice against Muslims.

In 2007 American public opinion was compared against public opinion in Great Britain, France, Italy, Spain, and Germany on "whether Muslims were a threat to National Security," whether Muslims in each of the countries "have become the subject of unjustified criticism and prejudice," whether Muslims have "too much, too little or the right amount of political power" in each of the countries, "Would you object if your child wanted to marry a Muslim," and "Do you have any friends who are Muslim?"

At 58 percent, the United States joined France and Germany in not believing Muslim Americans pose a threat to national security. At 47 percent, they joined France and Italy in believing that Muslim Americans have become the subject of unjustified criticism or prejudice. Only 34 percent of the Spanish public and 39 percent of the British public share that view. Less than 10 percent of the publics in any of the countries believe their Muslim community has little power. At 46 percent the British public has the highest percentage who believe Muslims have too much power, more than twice the percentage of the American public (20 percent).

At 40 percent, more Americans than any other group said they would object if their child wanted to marry a Muslim, and at 28 percent, Americans joined the Spanish in having the smallest percentage who said they have friends who are Muslims. All in all, the Americans' opinions were less hostile or negative than the British and less friendly and positive than the French, each of which were the two outliers.

The last survey also conducted in 2007 compared American public opinion toward the Muslim community against Jews, Catholics, Evangelical Christians, Mormons, and atheists. We found that about half of the public held favorable views of American Muslims and Mormons compared to three quarters who reported holding favorable views toward Jews and Catholics. Atheists were perceived favorably by only a third of the American public.

Gays and Lesbians

Questions posed in the earlier decades and included in the years 2005 to 2008, showed that between 49 and 59 percent of respondents thought homosexual relations between consenting adults should be legal. Between 48 and 57 percent thought homosexuality should be considered an acceptable alternative life style. Between 87 and 89 percent thought homosexuals should have equal rights in terms of job opportunities.

When asked whether homosexuality was something a person was born with or due to factors such as upbringing and environment between 46 and 54 percent answered "upbringing and environment" and "both."

On more recent items such as whether marriages between same-sex couples should or should not be recognized by the law as valid, between 53 and 59 percent thought they should not be valid.

And finally on a question asked between 2005 and 2008, "Would you favor a constitutional amendment that would define marriage as between a man and a woman thus barring marriage between gay and lesbian couples?" between 57 and 49 percent favored such an amendment, and between 37 and 48 percent opposed such an amendment.

On the military issue, which was asked again in 2007, 46 percent responded "serve openly," 36 percent responded "serve under the current policy," and 15 percent said "not serve under any circumstances."

Finally when asked between 2005 and 2008 about whether respondents would like to see homosexuality more or less widely accepted, or whether the acceptance level was about right responses were divided such that between 29 and 34 percent answered "more widely accepted," between 32 and 38 percent "less widely accepted," and between 27 and 30 percent answered "about right."

Immigrants

Between 2005 and 2008 more respondents, at between 16 and 18 percent, favored increasing immigration than at any time since the question was first asked in 1946. Thirty-nine percent favored maintaining the same level and 39 percent favored decreasing the number of immigrants admitted to the United States.

Between 54 and 43 percent said they were satisfied with the ways immigrants were treated. Between 74 and 79 percent thought the immigrants took low-paying jobs that American workers did not want. But 63 and 66 percent said immigrants cost tax payers too much.

When asked how satisfied they are with the treatment of immigrants in the United States, in 2005, 2006, and 2007 between 54 and 43 percent answered satisfied. In the most recent years, 2006 and 2007, less than a majority, 47 and 43 percent answered satisfied.

In 2006 and 2008, an item on illegal immigrants was included on national surveys:

"Do illegal immigrants pay their fair share of taxes?" to which a large majority, 63 percent in both years answered in the negative. Respondents believe illegals cost taxpayers too much.

But when asked whether illegal immigrants take jobs American workers want, 74 and 79 percent said illegals take low-paying jobs American workers don't want.

Finally, we found that between 61 and 67 percent of respondents believe that "On the whole, immigration is a good thing for the country today."

Abortion

In the most recent period when respondents were asked in 2006: "Under what circumstances do you believe abortion should be allowed?" at 31 percent, slightly less than a third answered "it should be permitted in all cases." And finally in 2008 when asked whether abortion should be legal, 19 percent said it should be legal in all cases, 38 percent said in most cases, 24 percent said it should be illegal in most cases, and 14 percent responded it should be illegal in all cases. We see that in 2008 a majority of the respondents, 57 percent, believed abortion should be legal in all or most cases.

And following up on those responses when asked in July 2008, "Do you support the *Roe v. Wade* decision?", 63 percent answered in the affirmative.

It is clear that *Roe v. Wade* still enjoys public support.

Affirmative Action

In 2008, the public was asked: "Do you think racism against blacks is or is not widespread in the U.S.?" Broken out by race, the results show that 51 percent of whites, 78 percent of blacks, and 59 percent of Hispanics thought racism was widespread.

Finally when asked in 2005 and 2007 "If two equally qualified students, one white and one black, applied to a major U.S. college or university who do you think would have a better chance of being accepted to the college?"

About half (48 and 50 percent) of the white respondents thought the two students would have the same chance, only 28 and 29 percent of the black respondents thought the two students would have the same chance, and among the black respondents 64 and 61 percent thought the white student would have the better chance of being accepted.

Notes

1.   Jefferson Morley. 2005. Israeli Withdrawal from Gaza Explained. *Washington Post*. August 10. Available through: *http://www.washingtonpost.com/wp-dyn/content/article/2005/08/10/AR2005081000713.html*. Access Date: December 11, 2008.
2.   BBC News. 2005. Israel Completes Gaza Withdrawal. September 12. Available through: *http://news.bbc.co.uk/2/hi/middle_east/4235768.stm*. Access Date: December 11, 2008.
3.   CNN.com. 2004. Bush praises Sharon's pullout proposal. April 15. Available through: *http://www.cnn.com/2004/WORLD/meast/04/14/bush.sharon/index.html*. Access Date: December 11, 2008.
4.   Stephen Zunes. 2007. The U.S. Role in the Gaza Tragedy. *Foreign Policy in Focus*. Available through: *http://www.fpif.org/fpiftxt/4331*. Access Date: December 11, 2008.
5.   Marcy Strauss. The Lessons from Abu Ghraib. Loyola Law School: Legal Studies Paper No. 2004-18. Available through: *http://ssrn.com/abstract=597061*. Access Date: December 12, 2008.
6.   *Op cit.*
7.   U.S. Supreme Court Media. Available through: *http://www.oyez.org/cases/2000-2009/2003/2003_03_6696/*. Access Date: December 13, 2008.
8.   Supreme Court of the United States. Available through: *http://www.cdi.org/news/law/rasul-decision.pdf*. Access Date: December 12, 2008.
9.   Nina Totenberg. 2006. Supreme Court Blocks Guantanamo Tribunals. NPR. Available through: *http://www.npr.org/templates/story/story.php?storyId=5520809*. Access Date: December 12, 2008.

10. U.S. Supreme Court. Available through:
http://www.supremecourtus.gov/opinions/07pdf/06-1195.pdf. Access Date: December 13, 2008.

11. Sayyid Imam's most recent theoretical revisions in 2008 titled "Al-Ta'reya le Ketab Al Tabre'a" (Revealing the Evils of AlTabre'a—a book written by Al-Zawahry) were published in a number of Arabic language newspapers including Al Masry Al-Youm and Asharq Alawsat.

12. National Oceanic and Atmospheric Administration. Hurricane Katrina—Most Destructive Hurricane Ever to Strike the U.S. Available through:
http://www.katrina.noaa.gov/. Access Date: December 12, 2008.

13. Spencer S. Hsu. 2006. Katrina Report Spreads Blame: Homeland Security, Chertoff Singled Out. *Washington Post.* 12 February. Available through:
http://www.washingtonpost.com/wp-dyn/content/article/2006/02/11/AR2006021101409.html. Access Date: December 12, 2008.

14. Alex Koppelman. 2005. Bush, race and social security. March 14. Salon.com. Available through:
http://www.salon.com/politics/war_room/2005/03/14/racists/index.html?calendar=200711. Access Date: December 13, 2008.

15. The White House. President Holds Press Conference. Available through:
http://www.whitehouse.gov/news/releases/2004/11/20041104-5.html. Access Date: December 13, 2008.

15

Concluding Comments

In these concluding remarks we report changes that have occurred in American attitudes on the topics discussed in each of the chapters from 1945 to 2008. For example, have Americans become more or less positive in their opinions about blacks, Jews, Muslim Americans, and gays and lesbians? Are they more or less favorable about admitting immigrants into the United States? Do they hold more or less favorable opinions about abortion and are they more or less likely to favor affirmative action programs?

Blacks

One of the earliest items to appear on national surveys (in 1942) about blacks questioned whether "Negros are as intelligent as white people," to which 42 percent answered yes. In 1963, 21 years later, 76 percent answered in the affirmative. On the matter of segregated schools in 1970, 24 percent of respondents living in the North objected compared to 43 percent of respondents living in the South. But on the issue of busing, in 1970, 78 percent of respondents nationwide indicated their opposition to "busing school children in order to achieve a better racial balance."

On the issue of desegregated public transportation, housing and employment opportunities attitudes moved in a pro-civil rights direction from 1945 onward. For example, on public transportation, opinions changed from 44 to 79 percent in favor of integration between 1942 and 1963. In 1963, 82 percent of respondents answered "yes" when asked whether Negros should have as good a chance as white people to get any kind of job.

When asked whether Negroes are treated fairly most white respondents from the 1940s through the 1960s said yes. But in 2001, only a little more than a third believed blacks were treated the same as whites. When asked specifically about whether blacks were treated the same as whites in their community by 1999, 76 percent thought they were. Finally, on some general issues, in 2001, 31 percent believed "black-white relations had improved over the last years." Forty-six percent rated "the state of race relations somewhat or very good." And when asked in 2007 to look into the future, 56 percent of white respondents said they thought the future of blacks will be better compared to 44 percent of black respondents. As of 2008 there is a big difference in white and black opinions about affirmative action programs with 39 percent of whites favoring them as opposed to 78 percent of black respondents.

Jews

Between the mid-1940s and 2007 the American public was asked whether they believed Jews have too much power in this country. In 1944 and 1946, 56 and 55 percent thought they did. By 2007, the percentage dropped such that only 15 percent thought Jews had too much power. And when asked whether they had heard any criticism or talk against Jews in the last six months, the percentage who answered that they had dropped from over 60 percent in the 1940s to 12 percent in 1959.

On the items that formed the Anti-Semitic Index that were asked between 1964 and 2002, on all of the items the responses indicated less anti-Semitic attitudes and more positive opinions about Jews over time. The items that showed the biggest differences were:

1) The trouble with Jewish businessmen is that they are so shrewd and tricky other people don't have a chance in competition.

In the 1960s between 40 and 54 percent held that view. In 2002, only 17 percent viewed Jewish businessmen in a negative light.

Along the same lines in 1964, 48 percent believed "Jews are more willing than others to use shady tactics to get what they want." In 2002, only 19 percent held that view.

In 1964, 48 percent thought "Jews have a lot of irritating traits," in 2002, the percentage dropped to 20.

On all of the items concerning attitudes toward Jews in the United States and Jewish qualities that were included on national surveys from 1945 to 2008, the American public's opinions about Jews shifted in a positive direction.

Muslim Americans

Items about attitudes toward Muslim Americans did not appear on national surveys until 2004. Between 2004 and 2007, four national surveys included items about Muslim Americans and Muslim communities in Great Britain, France, Italy, Spain, Germany, and the United States. In 2005, 55 percent of Americans reported favorable impressions of Muslim Americans, with blacks, persons under 30 years of age, college graduates, person with family annual incomes of more than $75,000, and liberal democrats holding the most favorable views.

When compared against Catholics, Jews, Evangelical Christians, and Atheists concerning respondents' favorable views, Jews and Catholics came out with a much higher percentage of favorable opinions. Muslim Americans and Evangelical Christians received lower and similar favorable views and Atheists received the lowest percentage of favorable views.

In 2006, about half of the respondents (49 percent) believed Muslim Americans were loyal to the United States.

When American opinions about the Muslim community in their country were compared against the Muslim community in Great Britain, France, Italy, Spain, and Germany on a variety of issues, the American opinions were less hostile or negative than the British and less friendly and positive than the French, each of which were the two outliers.

Gays and Lesbians

1977 was the first year that a question about homosexuality appeared on a national survey.

Do you think homosexual relations between consenting adults should be or should not be legal?

Between 1977 and 2008, that question was asked in 24 national surveys. In 1977, 43 percent of the American public thought homosexual relations between consenting adults should be legal. In 2008, 55 percent thought so. Over the years, the highest percentage who thought they should be legal was 60, in 2003.

And when asked on 14 national surveys between 1982 and 2008: "Do you feel homosexuality should be considered an acceptable alternative lifestyle or not?"

In 1982, 34 percent thought it should be an acceptable lifestyle. In 2008, the percentage increased to 57.

Another question on which there was a big shift of opinion was the following: "In general, do you think homosexuals should or should not have equal rights in terms of job opportunities?"

In 1977, 56 percent thought they should. By 2008, 89 percent thought they should.

Between 1977 and 2008, on 13 national surveys, when the public was asked: "In your view is homosexuality something a person is born with or is homosexuality due to factors such as upbringing and environment?"

The responses shifted from 13 percent in 1977 who thought homosexuality was something a person was born with to 41 percent who held that view.

On other items concerning attitudes and policies *vis-à-vis* homosexuality, *i.e.*, should marriage between same-sex couples be recognized by the law as valid, attitudes toward a constitutional amendment that would bar gay marriages, and whether respondents would like to see homosexuality more widely accepted, there were little shifts in opinions over time.

In sum, on those items on which there were big shifts in opinions, they were all in the direction of more favorable views *vis-à-vis* homosexuality.

Immigration

The basic question asked of the America public from 1946 to 2008 was: "Should U.S. immigration be kept at its present level, increased, or decreased?"

On the twenty-two times it appeared on national surveys, the percentage of respondents who favored increased immigration shifted from 4 percent to 18 percent. All of the responses in the double digits except for 1953 occurred between 1999 and 2008.

Immigrants who are viewed most positively are those who arrived early. Immigrants who are entering the country in large numbers at the time of the survey are viewed negatively. But on the whole, between 52 and 68 percent of the respondents said they thought immigration was a good thing for the country when the question was asked from 2001 to 2008.

On the matter of illegal immigrants on questions asked in 2006 and 2008, 66 and 63 percent of the respondents believed they cost the taxpayers too much, but 74 to 79 percent believe they take low-paying jobs American workers don't want.

On the whole, it is still fair to conclude that if public opinion dictated U.S. immigration policy, there would be many, many fewer immigrants admitted into the United States.

Abortion

The first national poll after *Roe v. Wade* conducted in 1975 revealed that 20 percent of the respondents believed abortions should be legal under any circumstances and that 20 percent believed abortions should be illegal under all circumstances. From 1975 through 1996, 25 percent favored legalizing abortions under all circumstances and 16 percent advocated making abortions illegal under all circumstances.

When asked in 2000, 2001, and 2003 whether abortion should be generally available less than 25 percent thought abortions should not be permitted.

On the most recent poll conducted in July 2008, 63 percent said they support *Roe v. Wade,* 33 percent oppose the decision. On abortion more generally, 19 percent said they believe abortion should be legal in all cases, 38 percent in most cases, 24 percent thought it should be illegal in most cases, and 14 percent in all cases.

The data show *Roe v. Wade* still enjoys wide support.

Affirmative Action

Between 1995 and 2003 when Americans were asked generally: "Do you favor or oppose Affirmative Action?" Between 58 and 63 percent said they did.

In 2003, 60 percent of the respondents said they thought affirmative action programs were good and 30 percent thought they were bad. But when asked about the fairness of the programs 47 percent said they thought they were fair and 42 percent thought they were unfair. By gender women were more likely than men to think they were good (65 v. 54 percent), and fair (52 v. 43 percent). By race, blacks (87 percent) were most likely compared to whites (54 percent) and Hispanics (77 percent) to think they were good. But Hispanics at 70 percent were most likely to think they were fair, compared to 58 percent of the black and 45 percent of the white respondents.

Differences in white and black perceptions are shown in the dramatic differences in responses to the following question:

> If two equally qualified students, one white and one black, applied to a major U.S. college or university who do you think would have the better chance of being accepted to the college?

Over 60 percent of the black respondents thought the white student would have the better chance compared to between 24 and 20 percent of the white respondents who thought the white student would have the better chance. Only 4 and 5 percent of the black respondents thought the black student would have the better chance, compared to between 24 and 34 percent of the white respondents who thought the black student would have the better chance.

When asked in 2003 who believed they have been personally helped or hurt by affirmative action programs, 84 percent of the white respondents said they were not affected by the programs. Two percent said they were helped and 13 percent said they were hurt. Among blacks, 77 percent said they were not affected, 14 percent said they were helped and 5 percent said they were hurt. Among Hispanics, 87 percent were not affected, 4 percent were helped and 8 percent were hurt. At least as of 2003 the large majority of respondents, irrespective of race or ethnicity, have not been affected by affirmative action programs.

Index

Page references followed by *t* indicate tables. Those followed by *n* indicate notes. Those in *italics* indicate illustrations.

Shiites, 159
Shuttlesworth, Fred L., 93
Sihanouk, Norodom, 112
Simpson, O. J., 151
Simpson-Mazoli Bill, 59
Sino-Soviet relations, 113
sit-ins, 92
sixties: between 1955 and 1964, 91–103;
   between 1965 and 1974, 105–19
Smith, John, 108
Social Security, 182
social spending, 147
Socialism, 137
Somalia, 148–49
South Africa, 138
South Carolina, 42, 53
South Dakota, 134
South Vietnam, 97
Soviet Union, 86, 96, 98; Berlin wall,
   97, 134; Cold War, 87, 91–103, 110,
   112–13; collapse of, 136; invasion of
   Afghanistan, 109, 113, 123–24; Moscow
   Summer Olympics (1980), 123; Sino-
   Soviet relations, 113
Spain, 36, 37t, 135, 164, 186–87, 193
Sputnik I, 98
Sputnik II, 98
Star Wars, 126, 158
stem cell research, 152
Stenberg v. Carhart, 68
Stevenson, Adlai, 87
Stith, Debora, 137
Stonewall riots, 106
Strategic Arms Limitations Treaty Agree-
   ments (SALT I), 113
Strategic Arms Limitations Treaty Agree-
   ments (SALT II), 113, 122–23
"strict scrutiny," 151
Student Nonviolent Coordinating Commit-
   tee (SNCC), 108
Students for a Democratic Society, 94
Sudan, 155
Suez Canal, 122
Suez crisis, 95
suicide bombings, 156
Summer Olympics (1980), 123
Sunnis, 159
Syria, 96, 110–11, 136

Taft-Hartley Act. *See* Labor-Management
   Relations Act

Taiwan, 113
Taliban, 154, 158
technology, 141, 183
Tehran, Iran, 123
terrorism, 140–41, 149, 154; 9/11 attacks,
   158; suicide bombings, 156; U.S. Em-
   bassy bombings, 126–27, 154–55; *USS
   Cole* bombing, 155; war on, 126–27
Tet offensive, 109
Texas, 42, 150, 161
Thatcher, Margaret, 136
Third Path, 137
Third War, 113
Third Way, 147
Three-Mile Island, 124
Time magazine, 110
Tiananmen Square massacre, 135
torture, 179–80
transportation: busing, 5–6, 6t, 99, 115;
   segregation on public transportation, 99;
   treatment of Negroes on buses, 15
Truman, Harry S., 85–86
Ture, Kwame, 108

Unified Task Force (UNITAF), 148
Union of Soviet Socialist Republics
   (USSR). *See* Soviet Union
UNITAF. *See* Unified Task Force
United Arab Republic, 96
United Nations, 111, 123, 126, 147–48,
   153–54
United Nations Special Commission (UN-
   SCOM), 153
United States: between 1945 and 1954,
   85–90; between 1955 and 1964, 91–103;
   between 1965 and 1974, 105–19; between 1975 and 1984, 121–32; between
   1985 and 1994, 133–41; between 1995
   and 2004, 147–76; between 2005 and
   2008, 177–90; citizenship requirements,
   54–55; Embassy bombings, 126–27,
   154–55; invasion of Iraq, 148; Muslims
   as threat to national security in, 36, 37t;
   public image of, 179
United States Commission on Civil Rights,
   138
United States Liaison Office (USLO),
   113
United States Navy, 155
United States Surgeon General, 137
University of Alabama, 93